(OLD) RAPPANANNOCK COUNTY, VIRGINIA

DEED and WILL BOOK ABSTRACTS
1665-1677

Ruth and Sam Sparacio

The Antient Press Collection
from

Colonial Roots
Millsboro, Delaware
2016

Colonial
Roots

Helping You Grow Your Family Tree

ISBN 978-1-68034-127-0

CONTENTS

(OLD) RAPPAHANNOCK COUNTY, VIRGINIA
Deeds & Wills No. 1
(1665-1677)

This Book is in two parts. The first part records Deeds, Bonds &c. dating from 5 July 1665 to February 22, 1665/6. The second part consists of Wills dating from 22 September 1672 to 2 May 1677.

On page 113 of the Original Book is the following entry: "All the records in this book were faithfully examined with the OLD RECORD BOOK by order of Essex County Court."

> by me W. BEVERLEY Cl Cur

There also is a Transcript of the complete book including both Deeds & Wills which includes pages 15 to 22 which are missing in the ORIGINAL BOOK. On page 224 of the Book of Transcript is the following entry:

> Memorandum:
> That what is contained in this Book from ye page 114 to this place is truely transcribed out of part of ye Book No. F and faithfully examined by me this vith day of July MDCCXXXI

> W. BEVERLEY Cl Cur

In the front of the ORIGINAL BOOK is an Index which lists both Deeds and Wills with page numbers relating to that book.

In the last part of the TRANSCRIPT BOOK is an Index which lists page numbers of both the ORIGINAL BOOK and the TRANSCRIPT BOOK.

All the entries given in our book are from the ORIGINAL BOOK with the exception of pages 15 to 22, which are taken from the TRANSCRIPT BOOK. Numbers of pages were deduced from the Index of the ORIGINAL BOOK. The TRANSCRIPT BOOK pages are numbered from 1 to 101.

SPARACIO

p.
1

I WILLIAM WEST do by these presents assigne over unto WILLIAM GIBSON for a valluable consideration received in hand all my right Interest and title of a third part of land which I WEST bought of FRANCIS TRIPLET & do by these presents sell & set over from me & my heirs unto WILLIAM GIBSON his heirs or assignes for ever as witness my hand December the 3rd 1664
Signed & sealed
in psence of us ENOCH DOUGHTY,   WILLM. WEST   Seal
    JAMES T GULLOCK his mark

pp.
1-
2

KNOW ALL MEN by these presents that I WILLIAM WEST of the County of Rappa: have by these presents nominated constituted & ordained my trusty & welbeloved friend ROBT. DAVIS my true & Lawfull Attorny for me & in my name to acknowledge in the next Court in Course a certaiane parcell of land sould by me to WILLIAM GIBSON being (torn) third part of a certain devident formerly bought by me of FRANCIS TRIPLET rattyfying confirming & allowing & holding for good what my sd Attorny shall herein act perform & do as if I myself were then & there personally present. Witness my hand & seal this 1st day of July 1665
Test ANTHONY MORGAN,   WILLIAM WEST   Seal
    JAMES T GULLUCK
Recognr in Cur Com Rappa 5d die July 1665
                 Test ROBT. DAVIS Cl Cur

p
2

I JOHN COOPR: of LONDON, Grocer, do constitute & appoint my loving Friend ALEXR: FLEMING my true & Lawfull attorney to ask and demand all such debts & demands as appears due to me from any persons whatsoever in Virga. & in default of paymt. to act in all cases & causes as any Attorney may or ought to do according to Law Witness my hand
Witness NICHO. COCK,   JOHN COOPER
    RICHD. BREDGAR, HENRY HASLEWOOD
Recordr in Com Rappa x die July 1665
                 Test ROBT. DAVIS Cl Cur pr du

p.
2

KNOW ALL MEN by these presents that I ROBERT TOMLINS do constitute & appoint my Friend Mr. RICHARD WEBLY my true & lawfull Attorny to act & doe fully in all respects for me & in my bussiness depending between me & Mr. JOHN COX fully as if I my self were there in person as witness my hand this 5th of July 1665
    THOS. FRESHWATER,   ROBT. T TOMLIN
    ROBT. GOODYEAR

pp.
2-
3

KNOW ALL MEN by these presents that I JOHN KILMAN doth freely give for me my heirs Exrs. one Cow calf unto JOHN BOUGHAN the Son of JAMES BOUGHAN his heirs Exrs marked as followeth the right Ear marked with one cropp & Slit & the left ear squared on the upper side & the sd JOHN BOUGHAN to enjoy the said Calf with all the increase male & female for him & his heirs as witness my hand this first day of March 1664
Test HENRY CREIGHTON   JOHN (blot) KILMAN
    JAMES I F FULLERTON
Recognitr in Cur Rappa 5 die July Ao. 1665

pp.   KNOW ALL MEN by these presents that I SILVESTER THACHER of the Parish of
3-   Sittingbourne in the County of Rappa: do for me my heirs Exrs or assignes con-
4   stitute ordaine & appoint my trusty & loving ffriend WILLIAM LANE of the
       Parish & County aforesd to be my true & lawfull attorny for me & in my name &
to my own use to sue implead & recover of JOHN AIRES of the County aforesd all & every
such sum & sums as shall lawfully appear to be due to me rattifying & confirming full
power unto my sd Attorney that whatsoever he shall doe in the Execution of the premises
or cause to be done I do hereby allow of as if personally present In Witness whereof I
have hereunto set my hand this 25th of Aprill 1665
Test JOHN RYMER,   SILVESTER ST THACHER
       WALTER x WILLIAMS

p.   KNOW ALL MEN by these presents that I JOHN PROSSER of the County of Rappa:
4   do constitute ordaine & appoint my welbeloved friend Mr. RICHARD WEBLEY to
       be my true & Lawfull Attorny for me & in my stead & place to answer all such
cause or causes as shall be entered agt: me or depending in the County Court above said
by Mr. RICHARD JAMES Giveing & by these presents granting unto my said Attorny as
full power in & about the premises as if I myself were personally present as Witness my
hand this 12th of May 1665
Test JOHN PAYNE,   JOHN PROSSER
       JOHN WAIGHT
Recordatr in Com Rappa: x die July 1665

                                              p ROBT. DAVIS Cl Cur pr da:

pp.   KNOW ALL MEN by these presents that I FRANCIS BROWNE do constitute & ap-
4-   point my Loving friend GEORGE DAVIS my true & lawfull Attorny for me & in
5   my Stead & behalf to appear in the County Court of Rappa: to answer unto all
       pleas Suits & demands which shall be objected agt. the said FRANCIS BROWN by &
in behalf of any person or persons suing & impleading me the sd FRANCIS BROWNE in
the County Court aforesaid as also to answer & prosecute all such business as shall belong to me, the sd FRANCIS BROWNE, in the sd Court hereby rattifying & confirming
whatsoever my said Attorney shall lawfully act & doe in the premises with as much
power & authority as if I myself did act & do the same in my own person. Witness my
hand & seal this tenth day of February 1664
Test THOMAS DANIEL,   FRANCIS BROWN   Seal
       THO: JENKINS

pp.   BE IT KNOWNE unto all men by these presents that I ELIZA. BROWN Now Wife of
5-   FRANCIS BROWN of PISCATACON in the County of Rappa: Planter have made con-
6   stituted ordained & deputed THOMAS JENKINS of the sd County Planter my true &
       lawfull Attorny for me & in my name place & stead to acknowledge in Court be-
fore his Matys Justices of the peace my free will & consent of in & concerning the Sale
of two hundred acres of land sould by the above named FRANCIS BROWN & I the sd
ELIZA. BROWN the Wife of sd FRANCIS as abovesd unto WILLIAM RICHARDS of the
abovesaid County Planter giving & granting unto my sd Attorney full power & lawfull
authority to act & doe herein for the better setling & confirming the sd Land unto the
sd WILLIAM RICHARDS all & every thing & things whatsoever which shall be thought
needfull & Expedient in & about the premises holding & by these presents confirming
whatsoever my sd Attorny shall do or cause to be done herein to all intentes and purposes as if myself were there in person present by virtue of these presents. In Witness whereof I the sd ELIZA. BROWN have hereunto set my hand & seale this thirtyeth

day of June in the year of our Lord One thousand Six hundred Sixty Five
Signed sealed & delivered
in presence of us WILLIAM PERRY,   ELIZA. ✗ BROWN Seal
　　　THOMAS ☿ EPER
Recognitr in Cur Com Rappa 5 die July Ao. 1665

pp.　KNOW ALL MEN by these presents that I JOHN DANDY Attorny of Mr. RICHARD
6-　GOWER of LONDON by Virtue of a Lettr. of Attorny from the sd Mr. RICHD. GOWER
7　　made to me JOHN DANDY above said bearing date the 21st day of Augt. 1663 have
　　　ordained constituted authorized & appointed & by these presents do ordaine constitute and appoint my Loving Friend JOHN CATLET my Lawfull attorny & do by these
presents give unto my sd Attorny the same & full power & authority in all respects to
act in any business belonging to the said Mr. GOWER as is by his Letter of Attorny in
any wise granted unto me. In Witness whereof I have hereunto set my hand & seal this
5th day of Aprill 1665.
Sealed Signed & delivered
in presence of us THOMAS LUCAS JUNR: JOHN DANDY   Seal
　　　WARWICK CAMMOCK
Recordatr: in Comr Rappa: 11 die 7bris Ao. 1665

pp.　KNOW ALL MEN by these presents that I RICHARD HINES of the County of Rappa:
7-　do by these presents give unto WILLIAM DANIEL to him or his heirs for ever
8　　one brown Cow marked with a slit down the left ear & two slits under the right
　　　ear with a brown Cow Calf of the same mark which Catle I give with their female
increase & do bind my self to look carefully after the sd Catle with their Increase aforesaid untill the said WILLIAM DANIEL comes to age & then to deliver them with an account of their increase but if in case the said WILLM. DANIEL should die before he
comes to age the Catle with their increase as afd. to go unto his Mother & whom she
pleases to give them to but if in case the sd WILLM: DANIEL live after he comes to be
Sixteen years of age the male increase of the afd. Catle to come unto him as well as the
female. In Witness of the truth I have hereunto set my hand & Seal the 4th of Septbr:
1665 & is to be recorded the next Court in Rappa: County
Signed Sealed in presence of us
　　　WILL. BARBER,   RICHD. ∦ HINES Seal
　　　WILLM. ✗ LUN
Recognr. in Cur Com Rappa 6 die 7bris Ao: 1665

pp.　KNOW ALL MEN by these presents that I DAVID MANSELL of the County of Rappa.
8-　in Virga. for & in consideration of the sum of Eight hundred pounds of tobo. in
9　　hand paid & received of JOHN JACOB do hereby bargaine & sell enfeoff & alienate
　　　& hath by these presents bargained sold enfeoffed & alienated unto JOHN JACOB
his heirs Exrs. Admrs. & assignes a tract or parcell of land containing One hundred
acres begining at a white Oak being a corner tree belonging to the land of RICHARD
POWELL & from thence runing for breadth alongst the side of the Swamp known by the
name of MADDISONS SWAMP & for leanth runing a mile into the woods, To have and to
hold to him the said JOHN JACOB his heirs Executors Admrs. & assignes for ever with
Ediffices & Emolumts. whatseover thereunto belonging without the let hindrance or
molestation of any person or persons whatsoever thereto belonging by for or under me
my heirs Exrs. Admrs. or assignes or any person or persons that may or shall lay or
make claime thereunto or any part thereof & in Testimony of all & singular the premises I have hereunto set my hand & Seal this 29th day of June 1665

Sealed & delivered in presence of us
        SAML. GRIFFIN,   DAVID MANSEL   seal
        LEROY GRIFFIN
Recognr in Cur Com Rappa 6 die 7bris Ao. 1665

pp.   KNOW ALL MEN by these presents that I Capt. DAVID MANSEL for a consideration
9-   in hand received hath by these presents made sale of a parcell of land from me
10   my heirs or assignes for ever firmly & by these presents from all person or
        persons whatsoever that may or can at any time lay any claime Title or interest
hereunto farther I the said DAVID MANSEL doth warrant grant unto ELDER ALDRIGE
thirty acres of land binding upon the head line of ROBT. FRISTOE Southerly to the
MOUNT FRAILES begining at a valley at a marked tree runing Southerly farther I the sd
DAVID MANSELL hath by the sd presents made over from me my heirs or assignes to
ELDER ALDRIGE his heirs or assignes firmly & by these presents to have & to hold the sd
Land for ever with all rights & priviledges whatsoever in as large & ample manner as
Law can maintaine & to the true performance hereof I set my hand & seal this 3d day of
September 1665
in presence of us GEORGE HOWELL   DAVID MANSELL   seal
        ROBT. ℞ FRISTO his mark
Recognr in Cur Com Rappa 6 die 7bris Ao: 1665

pp.   KNOW ALL MEN by these presents that I Capt. DAVID MANSELL of the County of
10-   Rappa: for & in consideration of Five thousand pounds of Tobacco & Cask in hand
11   already received by me DAVID MANSELL I DAVID MANELL have given & granted
        bargained sold aliened enfeoffed & confirmed & by these presents doe give
grant bargaine sell aliene enfeof & confirme unto GEORGE HOWEL his heirs Exrs. or
Assignes one parcell of land containing fifty acres of land begining upon the corner
tree of RICHARD POWELLs joyning to the land of ROBT. FRISTOEs & so runing up the
valley till I come to a marked tree that is marked on both sides of the valley from the
corner tree of RICHARD POWELL to these two marked trees in the valley I take for my
breadth & runing along the line of RICHARD POWELLs for my Leanth together withall
privildedges proffits commodityes Emolumts. & hereditamts. whatsoever thereunto belonging or appertaining. To have and to hold the sd land by these presents granted
unto the said GEORGE HOWELL his Wife & his Child their heirs Exrs. Admrs. peacably &
quietly to enjoy it for ever from all person or persons whatsoever as Witness my hand
& seal this Seventh of July 1665
Test ROBT. ℞ FRESTO,   DAVID MANSELL   seal
        MARY BRYAN ⧕ her mke
Recognr in Cur Com Rapa: 6 die 7bris 1665

p.   KNOW ALL MEN by these presents that I DAVID MANSELL of the County of
11   Rappahannock Gent do hereby authorize depute & ordaine & hath by these
        presents authorized deputed & ordained my Loving Friend SAML. GRIFFIN to be
my true & lawfull Attorny in my name & behalfe to acknowledge in Court the sale of the
parcells of land to the persons herein mentioned (to say) to JOHN JACOBS One hundred
acres; to GEORGE HOWELL fifty acres; & ELDER ALDRIDGEs thirty acres all which land
lying & being at the head of FARNHAM CREEK as by their sevll. conveyances may more
at large appear & what my sd Attorny shall act in & concerning the premises I do
hereby rattify & confirme in as full & ample manner to all intents and purposes in the
Law as if I my self were then & there personally present In Witness whereof I have
hereunto set my hand & Seale this 4th day of 7bris 1665

Witt   ROBT. ℟ FRESTO his mark   DAVID MANSELL   seal
       JOHN ⊣ ARNOLL his mark
Recordatr in Com Rappa: 11 die 7bris Ao. 1665

p.   KNOW ALL MEN by these presents that I JOHN PROSSER do ingage my self my
12   heirs Exrs. or Admrs. to make good assurance of one half of my Devident of land
       & plantation that I now live upon unto JOHN WAIGHT his heirs or assignes he or
they at Equall charge upon the same after ye other partys to whom I the said PROSSER
hath ingaged for land have their proportion laid out to the said WAIGHT paying unto
me the sd PROSSER p hundred acres as the other paid /that is to say/ seven hundred p
acres unto me the sd PROSSER my heirs or assignes but in case of the decease of either
party therefore know ye that the heirs Exrs. or Admrs. of either party shall Enjoy the
one half of the land plantation & housing in quantity & quality although it be not divided in the lifetime of either party notwithstanding the law to the contrary & also all
orcharding in the like case & to the true performance of the premises I have hereunto
set my hand & seal this tenth of March 1664
in presence of us SIMON MILLER,   JOHN PROSSER   seal
       WILLIAM VALE, ROBT. MAPES
Recognr in Cur Com Rappa 3 die Mai 1665

p.   I JOHN WAIGHT do acknowledge to assigne all my right title & interest of this
13   within specified Deed unto JOHN PROSSER his heirs or assignes for ever as wit-
       ness my hand & Seale this 16th of Augt. 1665
Signed & sealed in presence of us
       ALEX. FLEMING,   JOHN WAIGHT   seal
       JOHN LAMPART,   JEANE: WAIGHT
       ROGER ✗ RICHARDSON

p.   Moreover I JOHN WAIGHT do reassigne the sd Land from me & my heirs for ever
13   unto JOHN PROSSER & his heirs or assigns for ever Vizt. the Land mentioned &
       · acknowledged to me in Court May the 3d 1665 Witness my hand & Seal the day &
year abovesd.
in presence of ALEX. FLEMING,   JOHN WAYT   seal
       JOHN LAMPART, ROGER ✛ RICHARDSON
Acknowledged before us to be recorded p the use of JOHN PROSSER this 16th Augt. 1665
                                                  JOHN CATLET   predt.
                                                  ALEX: FLEMING Quo.
   The 16 day of September 1665 the sd JOHN CATLET & ALEX: FLEMING did in open Court
acknowledge & declare that the assignemt. or reassignmt. to this Instrument of
Writeing was acknowledged to & before them as is there mentioned
                                   Test   ROBT. DAVIS Cl Cur

pp.   KNOW ALL MEN by these presents that I JOHN PROSSER of the County of Rappa.
14-   Planter do by these presents acknowledge to have sold for the sum of Two thou-
15   sand pounds of tobacco & caske for divers considerations me hereunto moving
       the one half of my Plantation & housing & land thereunto belonging lying be-
tween ROGER RICHARDSONs line & the land of Mr. JOHN PAINE unto JOHN WAIGHT Planter of the same County /Vizt/ lying in the Freshes of Rappa. County upp on the North
West side of a Creek called the GOLDEN VALE & further I the said JOHN PROSSER do
acknowledge to give grant bargaine & sell aliene & confirm from me my heirs or Exrs.
unto JOHN WAIGHT his heirs or assigns for ever with a farther warranty from me or

any other person whatsoever claiming from by or under me my heirs or assignes for ever unto JOHN WAIGHT his heirs or assignes for ever he or they paying unto me my heirs or assignes or order such rents as are due to the Sacret Majesty or his Majestys Successors or Rent Gatherers for the one moiety to the true performance of the above-said premises according to all true intents & I have hereunto set my hand & seal this 26th of Augt. 1665

in presence of JOHN CATLET,			JOHN PROSSER			Seal
  ALEX. FLEMING,			MARTHA 𝆶 PROSSER		Seal
  JOHN LAMPART

(Note: Pages 15 to 22 are missing in the Original Book. Entries have been abstracted from the TRANSCRIPT BOOK pages 7 to 12.)

This Deed of Land was acknowledged before us by JOHN PROSSER and his Wife MARTHA PROSSER to be recorded for the use of JOHN WAIGHT and his heirs this 6d of Augt 1665
      JOHN CATLET
      ALEXR. FLEMING
 This 6 day of Septembr 1665 the sd JOHN CATLET and ALEXR. FLEMING did in open Court acknowledge and declare that this Deed of Sale was acknowledged before them by the said JOHN PROSSER and MARTHA his Wife for the use of the said JOHN WAIGHT

pp.	*(Page 8 Transcript).*
15-	KNOW ALL MEN by these presents that I JOHN PROSSER of the County of Rappa.
16	Planter do by these presents acknowledge to have sold for the sum of Fourteen
  hundred pounds of tobacco and cask and for divers considerations me hereunto
further moving Two hundred acres of land unto JOHN SPEARMAN Planter of the same County Vizt. lying in the Freshes of Rappa. County on the S. side the River begining at a white Oak at the mouth of a Creek called by name the GOLDEN VALE being a parcell of land belonging to a greater Patt. of JOHN PROSSERs and runing from the aforesaid white Oak into the woods with a line that parts the said land and the land formerly JOHN GIL-LETTs decd 320 p: SW thence through JOHN PROSSERs land: SW thence NE with the Miles End of GILLET thence NE to the side finally by the Creek to the place begun to say in all 200 acres that I JOHN PROSSER do acknowledge to give grant bargaine sell and confirm from me my heirs unto JOHN SPEARMAN his heirs for ever with further warranty from me or any other person claiming from by or under me my heirs or assigns unto JOHN SPEARMAN his heirs forever he the said JOHN SPEARMAN paying to me or my heirs or order such Rents as are due to me JOHN PROSSER and my heirs and to pay to his Sacred Maty or his Majestys Successors or Rent Gatherers for the sd 200 acres of land as is expressed in the Grand Pattent to the true performance of the abovesd premises according to all true intents and meaning I have hereunto set my hand and seal this (blank)

in presence of JOHN CATLET,			JOHN PROSSER			seal
  ALEXR. FLEMING,			MARTHA 𝆶 PROSSER		seal
  JOHN WAIGHT

 This Deed of Land was acknowledged before us by JOHN PROSSER and his Wife MARTHA to be recorded to the use of JOHN SPEARMAN and his heirs the 16 day of Augt 1665
      JOHN CATLET pt.
      ALEXR. FLEMING Quo.

 This 6th day of 7br 1665 the abovesd JOHN CATLETT and ALEXR. FLEMING did in open Court held for Rappa County acknowledge and declare that this Deed of Sale was ack-nowledged before them by the sd PROSSER and his Wife for the use of JOHN SPEARMAN and his heirs as is above expressed

                                             Test ROBT. DAVIS Cl Cur

pp.   *(Pages 8-9 of Transcript)*
17-   KNOW ALL MEN by these presents that I JOHN PROSSER of the County of Rappa
18   Planter do by these presents acknowledge to have sold for the sum of Two thousand Four hundred pounds of Tobacco and Cask and for divers considerations me
hereunto moving three hundred acres of land unto JOHN LAMPART Planter of the same
County lying on the Freshes of Rappahannock County on the South side of the River
begining at a white Oak that devides that abovesaid JOHN LAMPARDs land and the land
of JOHN SPEARMAN at the Mouth of a Creek in the Freshes of Rappa County called GOL-
DEN VALE CREEK and runing with SPEARMANs line SW thence NW at the foot of JOHN
SPEARMANs Second Mile thence S. W. to a North W. line of JOHN PROSSERs thence with
the said line NW thence SE butting on the land of JOHN SPEARMAN and finally NE to an
Ash standing by a small Pocoson to the Creek side to say in all three hundred acres.
Now Know yee that I JOHN PROSSER do acknowledge to give grant bargain sell and confirm from me my heirs or Exors. unto JOHN LAMPART and his heirs Exrors or assigns
for ever with further warranty of the said land with all rights and privileges thereunto belonging from me or any persons claiming from by or under me my heirs or
Exrs. or any other way unto JOHN LAMPART his heirs or assigns for ever said JOHN
LAMPART paying to me my heirs or Order such rents as are due to me JOHN PROSSER or
my heirs to pay to his sacred Maty or his Matys Successors or Rent Gatherers for the
abovesd three hundred acres of land is expressed in the Grand Pattent to the true performance of the abovesd premises according to all true intents and meaning, I JOHN
PROSSER do hereunto set my hand and Seal this 15th of Augt. 1665
in presence of JOHN CATLET.   JOHN PROSSER   seal
          ALEXR. FLEMING. JOHN WAIGHT
     This Deed of Land was acknowledged before us by JOHN PROSSER and his Wife MARTHA
to be recorded for the use of LAMPART and his heirs this 16th day of Augt. 1665
                                             JOHN CATLET
                                             ALEXR. FLEMING
     This 16th day of 7br 1665 the above said JOHN CATLET and ALEXR. FLEMING did in open
Court held for the County of Rappa acknowledge and declare that this Deed of Sale was
acknowledged before them by the sd PROSSER and his Wife MARTHA for the use of JOHN
LAMPART and his heirs as is above expressed
                                        Test   ROBT. DAVIS Cl Cur

p.   *(Pages 9-10 of Transcript)*
19   KNOW ALL MEN by these presents that I DOROTHY HOLT of the County of Rappa
          do covenant and condition to and with HENRY AUBREY Planter in the same
County for to live and dwell with the said HENRY AUBREY and his assigns from the day
of the date hereof for the full term of <u>Five years</u> in such service and employmt. as the
sd AUBREY shall imploy her excepting working in the ground, unless it be helping to
Plant in consideration whereof the said HENRY AUBREY is to find and allow the aforesd
DOROTHY HOLT sufficient diet washing and Lodging: Clothing during the term of <u>three</u>
years as aforesaid and furthermore the said HENRY AUBREY do bind and oblige himself
firmly by these presents to pay or cause to be paid unto ye abovesd DOROTHY HOLT one
Heifer with calfe or calfe by the side at the Expiration of the term of three years next
ensuing after the date hereof. In Confirmation whereof the sd DOROTHY HOLT and
HENRY AUBREY have set their hands for the performance of these premises above said

as Witness our hands this 27th of January 1663
In presence of N. JOHN POOLE,   DOROTHY *Ƌ* HOLT
        WILLIAM WILLIAMS   HEN: AUBERRY
Recordatr 11 die 7 anno 1665

pp.   *(Page 10 of Transcript)*
19-   TO ALL TO WHOM &c. Now Know ye &c. that I the sd Sr. WILLIAM BERKELEY Knt.
20   Governr. &c. do with the consent of the Councill of State accordingly give and
        grant unto RICHARD WEST and ROGER CLOTWORTHY Two hundred Eighty five
acres and a half of land lying on the South side of RAPPA RIVER beginning at a red Oak
being a corner tree of another Devident of the said WEST and extendeth itself parrallel
to the sd Devident S by E. to a marked white Oak nigh a branch thence E. by N. to a red
Oak on the West side of a valley thence S. by E. to a white Oak W. by S. to a red Oake nigh
a branch called POPEMANS CREEKE thence by or nigh the said branch N. W. to a red Oak
thence NW to a Pocickery Lastly E. by N. to the place where it began, the said land being
due unto the said WEST and CLOTWORTHY by and for the transportation of Six persons
into this Colony whose names are on the records mentioned underneath this Pattent to
have and to hold &c. Given at JAMES CITY under my hand and the seal of the Colony this
28th day of July 1663 and in the 14th year of the Reign of our Sovereign Lord KING
CHARLES ye second &c.
R. WEST and ROGER CLOTWORTHY   WILLIAM BERKLEY
their Pattent for 285 acres and 1/2 of land

  KNOW ALL MEN by these presents that I ROGER CLOTWORTHY for a valuable consideration in hand received do from my self and my heirs assign unto CATLET his heirs and
assigns all my right title and interest of one half of the within mentioned Pattent and
Land containing in all Two hundred Eighty five acres an half of land (Vizt) the one
half of the same lying on the upper side of ye line of marked trees that divides the said
land in two parts. In Witness whereof I have hereunto set my hand and seal this 25th
day of June 1665
in presence of us JOHN CATLETT,   ROGER *ᏒᏋ* CLOTWORTHY   seal
        DANL. GAINES
Recognr in Cur Com Rappa 6 die 7bris Anno 1665

p.   *(Page 11 of Transcript)*
21   KNOW ALL MEN by these presents that we ROGER CLOTWORTHY and LIDIA CLOT-
        WORTHY have constituted and appointed and do by these presents constitute and
appoint our loving friend Capt. ALEXR. FLEMING our lawfull Attorney in our names to
acknowledge in Court our Voluntary consent in the Sale of our right and title of the one
half of the Pattent and the Land contained therein granted unto me the abovesaid
ROGER CLOTWORTHY and RICHARD WEST the said half part of land to acknowledge the
Sale thereof to NICHOLAS CATLET according to assignmt. on the back of the sd Pattent.
In Witness whereunto we the abovesaid have set our hands and seals this 29th day of
June 1665
Test JOHN CATLET   ROGER *ᏒᏋ* CLOTWORTHY
        JANE GULLOCK p signe   LIDIA *ϒ* CLOTWORTHY
Recordtr 11 die 7bris Anno 1665

p.   *(Page 12 of Transcript)*
22   KNOW ALL MEN by these presents that I JAMES FULLERTON do give unto my
        Daughter ELIZABETH One Cow and a yearling Heifer called by the name of

Nanny marked the swallow fork on the right ear and a piece taken out underneath the
swallow fork and a crop on the left ear this Cattle above mentioned I the above named
JAMES FULLERTON do give unto my Daughter with all the female cattle that they shall
breed as Witness my hand this 6th day of Septembr in the year of our Lord God 1665
Test HENRY CREIGHTON   JAMES ‡ Ŧ FULLERTON
          JOHN ⅃ LONG
Recognr in Cur Com Rappa a 6 die 7bris Ao. 1665

  JAMES FULLERTON his mark is as followeth a swallow fork on the right ear and a cross
an crop and an underkeel on the left ear this mark above named I JAMES FULLERTON
do acknowledge to be my proper mark
Recordatr 11 die 7bris Ao. 1665

p.   KNOW ALL MEN by these presents that I WILLIAM HODGKINS do constitute or-
23   daine and appoint my trusty and well beloved Friend Mr. GEORGE DAVIS to be my
         true and lawfull attorny for me and in my behalf to answer what suits shall be
commd. agt me in Rappa. Court. I do authorize and impower my said Attorney to act and
doe in my behalf as expressly in the premises in as full and ample manner as if I
myself were personally present Justifying and confirming whatever my sd Attorney
shall lawfully do as Witness my hand and seal this 3d day of September 1665
Test JOHN MEADER,   WILL. HODGKINS   seal
          MARY ELSHER

p.   The Mark of NICHOLAS CONSTABLE Vizt: a crop on the right ear & a slit on the
23   crop & a nick under the left being the proper mark of Hoggs & Catle 11d 7br
          1665
Recordatr.   p RT R. D. Cl Cur

pp.   KNOW ALL MEN by these presents that I HENRY CREIGHTON of the County of
24-   Rappa. in Virga. by & with the Consent of FRANCIS my Wife for divers good
25   causes & valuable considerations us thereunto moving & more especially for the
          sole consideration of one Cow Calfe already delivered to me by WILLIAM BRUCE
of the same County have granted sold & confirmed & do by these presents give sell &
confirme unto the sd WILLIAM BRUCE his heirs & assignes Two acres & thirty four
perches of land situate lying & being in the aforesaid County & on the North side of
RAPPA. RIVER being part of a Devident of land whereon I the said CREIGHTON now live
together with all the houses edifices & buildings & appurtenances thereunto belonging
begining at a marked Stump in the North & South lines that divides the lands of the said
CREIGHTON & the said BRUCE N. unto a marked Pocickory that standeth in the Division
lyne thence SSW half a point westerly to a marked Stump thence S. by West to the East
lyne thence to the place where begun East 14 poles to have & to hold the said Two acres
& thirty four perches withall the houses Edifices buildings & appurtenances to him the
sd WILLIAM BRUCE his heirs admrs. or assignes for ever to the sole & proper use of him
the sd WILLIAM BRUCE his heirs & assigns forevermore the sd WM. BRUCE paying &
discharging the rights & services therefore first due & of right accustomed & furthermore I the said HENRY CREIGHTON & FRANCES my Wife do for us our heirs & admrs. promise & grant with the sd WILLIAM BRUCE his heirs & assignes that he the said WILLIAM
BRUCE his heirs or assignes shall & may from time to time and at all times hereafter
quietly enjoy the sd two acres & thirty four perches of land with the aforementioned
pmises without any hindrance of us the said HENRY & FRANCES or any other person
lawfully claiming the same. In Witness whereof we the sd HENRY & FRANCES have

hereunto set our hands & seals this 25th of May 1665
in presence of us ALEXR. FLEMING   HENRY CREIGHTON   seal
       ROBT. DAVIS   FRANCIS CREIGHTON   seal
Recognr in Cur Com Rappa 6 die 7bris Ao. 1665

pp.
25-
26

KNOW ALL MEN by these presents that I ROBT. SISSON do make ordaine constitute & appoint my welbeloved Friend WILLIAM LOYD to act on my behalf in any
matters & causes which may any ways concerne me at the next Court held for
this County of Rappa: rattifying & confirming whatsoever my sd Attorny shall
lawfully act in the premises giving & granting to my sd Attorny as full power as any
Attorny might or may have in such cases Witness my hand this 4th: of September Ao:
Dom: 1665
Witness hereunto WILLIAM LANDMAN   ROBERT SISSON
       The marke of THOMAS CLOVDALE
Recordatr 11 die 7bris Ao: 1665

pp.
26-
27

THESE PRESENTS Witnesseth that I THOMAS DIOS of the County of WESTMORELAND
in Virginia do constitute ordaine & appoint my Friend THOMAS FRESHWATER to
be my true & lawfull attorny for me & in my name & steed to answer to all such
cause & causes as shall be entered agt. me in the County Court of Rappa: by JOHN
PAINE of the said County as also to ask demand sue for recover & receive all & singular
such debt or debts as may appear due to me by Bill from ROBT. SMITH of the abovesd
County deced giveing & by these presents granting unto my sd Attorny as full power in
& about the premises abovementioned as if I myself were personally present as Witness
my hand this 1st: day of September 1665
Test RICHARD BRAMHAM,   THOMAS DYOS
       SAML: $\mathcal{SB}$ BOWIN
Recordatr in Com Rappa 11 die 7bris Ao: 1665

p.
27

MEMORANDM: I JOHN PROSSER do acknowledge by these presents that the Two
hundred acres of land within specified & sold by me unto JOHN SPEARMAN is
part of a Pattent taken out of the Office & due to me in the year 1660 the 20th day
of July & that I do according to all true intents & meaning warrt. the sd Land from that
date unto JOHN SPEARMAN & his heirs & assignes from me & my heirs for ever Witness
my hand this 20th day of January 1665
Signed sealed & delivered &   JOHN PROSSER   Seal
   Acknowledged to be recorded before us
   the day abovesaid JOHN CATLET
           ALEXR. FLEMING
Recordatr in Com Rappa 12 die 7bris 1666

pp.
27-
28

MEMORANDM. that I JOHN PROSSER do acknowledge by these presents that the
three hundred acres of land within specified & sold by me unto JOHN LAMPART
is part of a Pattent of Land taken out of the Office due to me in the year 1660 the
20th: day of July & that I do according to all true intents & meaning Warrant the
sd Land from the date unto JOHN LAMPART & his heirs & assignes from me & my heirs
for ever Witness my hand this 20th day of January 1665
before us the day abovesd   JOHN PROSSER   seal
   JOHN CATLET
       ALEXR. FLEMING
Recordatr in Com Rappa 12 die 7bris 1665

pp.   KNOW ALL MEN by these presents that I JOHN PROSSER of the County of Rappa:
28-   Planter do by these presents acknowledge to have sold for the sum of Two
29   thousand four hundred pounds of tobacco & cask & for divers considerations me
thereunto moving three hundred acres of land unto ROGER RICHARDSON of the
same County Vizt: lying in the freshes of Rappa: County on the South side of the River
begining at a small Ash neer a pocoson & runing into the woods by a line of trees that
parts him & JOHN LAMPART SW Westerly to a NW Line of JOHN PROSSERs thence NW to
the place the land begun at Ye Ash neer the Creek called the GOLDING VALE CR: Now
Know ye that I JOHN PROSSER do with the free consent of MARTHA my Wife acknowledge to give & grant & sell from me my heirs for ever & from the Dower of my Wife
unto ROGER RICHARDSON & his heirs & assigns for ever with all rights & priviledges
thereunto belonging with further warranty of the sd Land from me or any persons
claiming under me my heirs or assignes for ever to he the sd ROGER RICHARDSON or
assigns paying to me or my heirs or assignes such rents as are due to be paid to his
Sacret Majesty or his Successors or Rent Gatherers for the abovesaid Land as is
Expressed in the Grand Pattent to the true performance of the sd Sale according to all
true meaning I JOHN PROSSER with MARTHA my Wife do hereunto set our hands & seals
this 28th of October 1665

in presence of ALEXR. FLEMING,   JOHN PROSSER   seal
        RO: TALIAFER   MARTHA ᛗ PROSSER   seal
Recognr in Cur Com Rappa primo die 9bris Ao. 1665

pp.   I MARTHA PROSSER the true & lawfull Wife of JOHN PROSSER of Rappa: County
29-   in Virga: do constitute & appoint my Loveing Friend Capt. ALEXR. FLEMING my
30   lawfull Attorny to acknowledge a Deed of land sold by my Husband with my con-
       sent to ROGER RICHARDSON cont. 300 acres having received satisfaction for the
same. In Witness whereof I have hereunto set my hand & seal this 28th of October 1665
                                        MARTHA ᛗ PROSSER   seal

p.   TO ALL TO WHOM &c. Now Know ye &c. do with the consent of the Councell of
30   State accordingly give & grant unto MILES REYLEY one thousand acres of land
       on the North side of the RAPPAHANOCK RIVER begining at a red Oak runing E.
by So. from a marked red Oak N. by W. containing in all One thousand acres the said
Land being due unto the sd MILES REYLEY by & for the transportation of Twenty persons into this Colonly whose names are on the records mentioned underneath this
Pattent, To have and to hold &c.: To be held &c: yealding & paying &c: Provided &c:
Given at JAMES CITY under my hand & the Seal of ye Colony this 12th day of October
1665 &c.
                        WILLIAM BERKLEY

pp.   KNOW ALL MEN by these presents that I JOHN HULL of the County of Rappa: in
30-   Virga: for a valuable consideration me thereunto moveing do from me my heirs
31   & assignes transfer & make over all my right title & interest of the within men-
       tioned Pattent & land therein mentioned unto FRANCIS SUTTLE his heirs Exrs
Admrs or assignes forever as Witness my hand & Seale this first day of 9ber 1665
                                        JOHN HULL   seal
Recognr in Cur Com Rappa: primo die 9bris 1665

pp.   TO ALL TO WHOM &c. Now Know ye that I the said Sr. WILLIAM BERKLEY Knt:
31-   Governour &c. do with the consent of the Councel of State accordingly give &
32   grant unto Mr. THOMAS CHETWOOD & GEORGE HASELOCKE Two thousand two hun-

dred & fifty acres of land lying on the North side of Rappa: County & bounding as fol-
loweth: runing along a Maine Branch at the head of TOTOSKEY CREEK called the CROSS
CREEK runing for breadth South upon the Maine Branch 640 poles from a marked white
Oak East into the woods 640 poles from a marked red Oak North 560 poles from a marked
red Oak West 340 poles to a Chesnut that divides this land & the land of Mr. SAMUEL
GRIFFIN & so to the place where it first begun the sd Land being due to the said CHET-
WOOD & HASLELOCK by & for the transportation of 45 persons into this Colony whose
names are on the records mentioned underneath this Pattent, To have and to hold &c. To
be held &c. Yealding & paying &c. Provided &c. Given at JAMES CITY under my hand &
the Seal of the Colony this 9th day of July 1665 &c.

WILLIAM BERKLEY

p.   KNOW ALL MEN by these presents that I THOMAS CHETWOOD of the County of
32   LANC: for & in consideration of the quantity & moiety of Five hundred acres of
        land made over to me by Mr: WILLIAM TRAVERS of Rappa: County as also the
sum of Three thousand pounds of tobacco & cask the receipt whereof I do acknowledge
have given sold & confirmed & by these presents do give sell & confirme the whole
contents of the within mentioned Pattent land in this Pattent unto the said WM. TRA-
VERS his heirs Exrs. or assignes for ever to have and to hold the abovesaid premises
with every part & parcell thereof with all right & proffits as is therein to me granted
from me the sd CHETWOOD my heirs admrs. or assignes or any other person whatsoever.
Witness my hand & seal this 2d: day of November 1665
in presence of us ALEX: FLEMING,   THO: CHETWOOD
        THO: HAWKINS
Recognr in Cur Com Rappa secundo die 9bris Aó. 1665

pp.   THIS INDENTURE made the 10th day of Octr: in the year of our Lord God 1664 Be-
33-   tween PETER JOHNSON of the County of Rappa: & Parish of Sittingbourne Planter
34   of the one partie & the VESTRY of the PARISH aforesd on the other party Wit-
        nesseth that the sd PETER JOHNSON for & in consideration of the sum of five
hundred pounds of good lawfull tobacco in hand received of the PARISH aforesd hath
given sold & made over & doth by these presents fully give & make over from him the
said PETER JOHNSON his heirs & Successors four acres of land with the appurtenances
set lying and being in the Parish aforesaid & on the South POINT that maketh the mouth
of a Creek called OCCUPACY & to be laid out as neer as may be Square on the sd POINT the
same to have and to hold from the date hereof for ever & further that the sd PETER
JOHNSON his heirs or assignes shall & will before the last day of November next or
sooner if thereunto lawfully called by the PARISH or VESTRY of the same make & execute or cause to be made a good sure rightfull perfect absolute & lawfull estate in the
Law of the said land to the only proper use of the said Parish for ever with warranty
agt: all men whatsoever by from or under him claimeing or pretending any claime to
any part or parcell thereof. In Witness that this is his Free voluntary act he hath
hereunto set his hand & seale ye day & year above specified
in presence of us W. MOSELEY,   PETER ⊕ JOHNSON   seal
        XPER ✚ CHAUNT, JOHN DEANE
Recognr in Cur Com Rappa 2 die 9bris Ao. 1665

p.   I PETER JOHNSON of the County of Rappa: & Parish of Sittingbourne do by these
34   presents authorize & depute Capt. JOHN HULL of the same County & Parish of
        Farnham my lawfull attorny for me & in my steed & place to acknowledge in this
sd County Court held ye second day of November next all my right title & interest of in &

to four acres of land lying in ye said Parish of Sittingbourne afd. which I acknowledge
to have sold to the sd PARISH of SITTINGBOURNE as Witness my hand this 18th day of
November 1665

Test JOHN WEIR,   PETER ⊕ JOHNSON
    ROBT: DAVIS
Recordatr x die 9bris 1665

pp.   TO ALL TO WHOM &c. Now Know yee &c. that I the sd FRANCIS MORRISON Esqr: &c
34-   do with the consent of the Councell of State accordingly give & grant unto
35   WILLIAM KILLMAN one hundred Sixty four acres of land situate lying on the
    Eastermost side of PISCATACON CREEK in the County of Rappa: & begineth at a
marked Spanish Oak at the head of a Cove & nigh adjoining to the uppermost Corner
tree of the land of JOHN CAPELL by the aforesaid Creeks side thence extending itself East
South East to a small pisimond tree in a Swamp thence South South East through part of
the said Swamp up the Hills to a marked red Oak on falling ground thence SW being the
course parellel to the Creek to a marked white Oake on a Levell betwixt two branches
being the corner tree of the Land of JNO. & GEORGE KILLMAN at their first miles end
thence by their line North West down to the aforesd Creeks side & so with the sd Creek
to the tree first above mentioned ye sd land being due unto him by & for the Transportation of Four persons into this Colony whose names &c. to have &c. to be held &c.
yealding & paying &c Provided &c Given at JAMES CITY under my hand & the seal of the
Colony this 15th day of June 1661

Recordatr 10th June 1665   FRANCIS MORRISON
    Test PHIL LUDWELL Cl Offe: THO: LUDWELL Secr:

pp   KNOW ALL MEN by these presents that I within named WILLIAM KILLMAN for &
35-   in consideration of Two thousand pounds of Merchble Tobacco to me in hand
36   paid at & before the ensealing & delivery hereof by JOHN HULL gent well & truly
    paid the receipt whereof I do hereby acknowledge & thereof clearly discharge
the sd JOHN HULL his Exrs. & assignes have sold & confirmed & by these presents do for
me my heirs Exrs: fully & absolutely grant sell & confirme unto the sd JOHN HULL his
heirs Exrs or assignes all & singular that One hundred & sixty four acres of land within
mentioned or intended to be given granted to me with all rights & priviledges appurtenances the same to have & to hold the sd one hundred Sixty & four acres of land with
all rights as aforesd unto the sd JOHN HULL his heirs & assignes with warranty of &
from all & every person whatsoever by these presents. In Witness whereof I have
hereunto set my hand & Seal the 6th day of March Ao. Dom 1664

in presence of THO: FRESHWATER,   WILLM. T KILMAN   seal
    JO. TAVERNOUR
Recognr in Cur Com Rappa: 2 die 9bris Ao: 1665

p.   KNOW ALL MEN by these presents that I WILLIAM KILMAN have nominated
37   made ordained & by these presents do put & constitute my loving Friend THOMAS
    FRESHWATER my Lawfull Attorny for & in my name to appear before the Wor-
shipfull Justices of the Peace of the County of Rappa: & there to acknowledge all my
right & interest of & to one hundred Sixty and four acres of land unto JOHN HULL his
heirs & assignes according to the purport of a certaine Indenture bearing date with
these presents Witness my hand & Seal the 6th day of March 1664

in presence of RANDAL KERKE,   WILLIAM T KILLMAN seal
    JO: TAVERNOUR
Recordatr x die 9bris 1665

pp.   WHEREAS by his Majestys Royall Comission bearing date the last of Augt: 1664
37-   I am constituted & deputed AUDITOR GENL: of all Publick Accompts in his Matys
38   Colony of Virginia with full power & authority amongst other matters & things
      in the sd Comission expressed to sumon all SHERIFFs & other Collectors of the
Levys & Quitrents to appear before me at JAMES CITY at such time & times as I shall
think most convenient then to render me a perfect acct: of their severall receipts &
disbursemts. of the sd Publick Levys & accordingly take out their respective discharges
from my Office in JAMES CITY aforesd
  THESE ARE therefore in his Matys name to will & require you the Sheriffs and Collec-
tors of Rappa: for the time being to make your personall appearance before me at the
place aforesaid from the 20th to the 25th of March & those that are then deficient to
appear between the 20th and 23th of May annually then & there to give up your
severall accts: & to take out your discharges in manner & form aforesd & hereof you are
not to fail as you will answer the contrary as Contemners of his Matys Royall Command
Given under my hand this 24th of October 1665
                                        THOMAS STEGGE   Audr:
Recordatr x die 9bris 1665

pp.   We whose name are hereunder written being VESTRY MEN for the PARISH of
38-   SITTINGBOURNE & FARNHAM do here unanimously agree for the future main-
39   tenance of Mr. FRANCIS DOUGHTY Minister the two next Ensuing years & it is
      agreed upon as followeth that Mr. FRANCIS DOUGHTY shall receive yearly of
each Parish abovesd Sixty pounds Sterling to be paid in Tobacco according to act of
Assembly ye sd tobacco to be paid in Cask without Sallery or other charge to the sd Mr.
DOUGHTY hereby revokeing & dissannualling all former orders bargains & Contracts
whatsoever made by & between the said Mr. FRANCIS DOUGHTY & both or either the
respective VESTRYs of the Parishes aforesaid to the true performance of which the said
Mr. FRANCIS DOUGHTY & the VESTRY of both Parishes have hereunto set their hands
this 3 day of November Ao. 1665:

        FRA: DOUGHTY   FRA: DOUGHTY
        THOM: GOODRICH   JOHN CATLET
        JOHN GRIGGORY   ALEXR. FLEMING
        THO: BUTTON   JOHN WEIR
        ROBT. ℛℬ BAYLEY   THOS: HAWKINS
        JAMES SAMFORD   HUM: BOOTH
        THOS: ℛ ROBINSON   W. MOSELEY
        ANT. NORTH   JOHN PAINE

Recognr in Cur Com Rappa 3 die 9bris Ao. 1665

pp.   KNOW ALL MEN by these presents that I ROBT: MOSS do hereby acknowledge to
39-   have sold & conveyed from me my heirs Exrs. or assignes a parcell of land
40   lying & being upon the Maine Branch of a Swamp called by the name of
      CHESTUCKSENT & bounden with marked trees under the HILLS to a marked white
Oake marked three ways in the line & thence Extending it self to the miles end of my
Devident being the Quantity of One hundred acres either more or less the sd land being
made over as is aforesaid unto RICHARD STOAKES his heirs or assigns for ever with all
rights & priviledges thereunto belonging in as full & ample manner as it is granted to
me by my Pattent the sd Land being part of a tract of land sold to me by Mr. WILLIAM
MOSELEY he the sd RICHARD STOAKES being lyable from henceforth to pay his Matys
quitrents & all taxations that shall be demanded as Witness my hand & Seal this 29th of

January 1664
Test JOHN LAMPART,   ROBT: MOSS   seal
     PETER ◯ JOHNSON

I REBECKA MOSS do give my full & free consent to ye sale of this Land abovementioned
as Witness my hand this 20th Jan: 1664
Test JOHN LAMPART,   REBECCA ⫯ MOSSE   seal
     PETER ◯ JOHNSON

p.   I REBECKA MOSS make STEPHEN CATOR my full & lawfull Attorny for the Sale of
41   the Land within the mentioned Conveyance. Witness my hand the 20th of
       October 1664
       GRIFFIN JONES,   REBECCA ⫯ MOSSE
        DAVID TUCKER
Recognr in Cur Com Rappa 2 die 9bris 1665

p.   JAMES CITY 23d: 8br 1665
41   It is ordered that Capt: HUMPHRY BOOTH be added to the COMISSION of Rappa:
       County & to take his place as a Justice of the peace in the sd Comission as for-
       merly to be sworne at the next County Court there held
                                              By the Governours Comand
                                                  FRA: HICKMAN Cl Cur

Recorded x die 9bris 1665

pp.   THIS INDENTURE made the 29th: of October in the year of our Lord God 1665 &
41-   the Reign of our Sovereign Lord the King the 17th: Between THOMAS RAWSON of
43   the County of Rappa. Planter & STUBBLE STUBLESON of the same County Planter
       Witnesseth that the sd THOMAS RAWSON for & in consideration of One thousand
pounds of good & lawfull tobacco with cask by him in hand received of the sd STUBLES
hath granted sold & made over from him the sd RAWSON his heirs and Successors all the
land belonging to him by Pattent bearing date the Eighteenth day of November 1663
containing 503 acres & 4 perches only excepting to himself & his heirs forever his now
Plantation & a small parcell of Woodland adjacent thereunto being marked out in presence of several of the neighbourhood to STUBLE STUBLESON his heirs & Successors for
ever with the appurtenances sett & being in the County aforesaid & in the Parish of
Sittingbourne & on the North side of ye MILL BRANCH being ye head of TIGNERS CREEK
the same to have & to hold to him & his heirs for ever & further the sd THOMAS RAWSON
or his heirs or assignes shall & will at the next Court held for this County if thereunto
lawfully called by the sd STUBLES or any by him assigned make & execute a good sure
rightfull perfect & lawfull Estate in ye Law of the sd Land to ye only & proper use of the
said STUBLES & his heirs for ever only excepting ye aforementioned parcell to his own
use with warranty agt. all men whatsoever by from or under him claiming or pretending any claime to any part thereof only ye aforementioned parcel excepted. In
Witness that this is his own free & voluntary act he hath hereunto set his hand & seal
the day & year above written & the said RAWSON hath excepted fencing Stuff for his
own proper use on the NECK Between the GUNN SWAMP & the SPRING BRANCH for his
life time
in presence of us W. MOSELEY,   THOMAS RASON   seal
     JOHN DEANE
Recognr: in Cur Com Rappa 3 die 9bris Ao. 1665

pp.   THIS INDENTURE made the 6th day of January in the year of our Lord Christ 1659
43-   Witnesseth that BARTHOLOMEW CLARKE ye Son of JOHN CLARKE of the City of
45   CANTERBURY, Sadler, of his own likeing & with ye Consent of FRANCIS PLUMER
of ye City of CANTERBURY, Brewer, hath put himself apprentice unto EDWARD
ROUZEE of Virga. Planter as an apprentice with him to dwell from ye day of date above
mentioned unto ye full end & term of four years from thence next ensuing & fully to be
compleat & ended all which sd terme the sd BARTHOLOMEW CLARKE well and faithfully
the sd EDWARD ROUZEE as his Master shall serve his secrets keep his commandmts. just
& lawfull he shall observe & fornication he shall not comit nor contract matrimony
within any woman during the sd Terme he shall not do hurt unto his said Master nor
consent to ye doing of any but to his power shall hinder & prevent ye doing of any at
Cards dice or any unlawfull games he shall not play he shall not waste the goods of his
sd Master nor lend them to any body without his Master's consent he shall not absent
himself from his sd Masters service day nor night but as a true & faithfull Servt. shall
demean & behave himself the sd EDWARD ROUZEE in ye mistery art or occupation of a
Planter which he now useth after the best manner he can the sd BARTHOLOMEW to
teach or cause to be taught & also during ye sd Terme shall find & allow his sd Apprentice competent meat drink apparel washing Lodging with all other things fitting for
his degree & in the end thereof fifty acres of land to be laid out for him & all other
things which according to the Custom of the Country is or ought to be done. In Witness
whereof the partys to these presents their hands interchangeably have set ye day &
year first above written
in presence of us WILLM. BROWN.   BARTHOLOMEW *BC* CLARKE seal
      ROBERT CUMBERLAND
Recordatr x die 9bris 1665

p.   KNOW ALL MEN by these presents that I STUBLE STUBLESON of the County of
45   Rappa: Planter doe hereby acknowledge to have sold to THOMAS RAWSON one
   black Cow with a litle white under her belly named Dary crop on the left ear & a
nick under the crop & a swallow fork & hole on ye right & one red Heiffer three years
old named Cherry cropt on the left ear & a nick under the crop & the right ear whole
them to be & to belong with their Increase to the sd RAWSON or his Order & I do hereby
warrt: the said sale to be good honest & lawfull & that the sd Catle did at ye Subscribing
hereof properly belong unto me & no person as Witness my hand this 29th 8br 1665
Test W. MOSELEY,   STUBLES ++ STUBLESON
Recognr in Cur Com Rappa 2 die 9bris Ao. 1665

pp.   TO ALL TRUE XPIAN People to whom this present wrighteing shall come sendeth
45-   greeting in our Lord God Everlasting Know ye that HUMPH: BOOTH of Rappa:
47   County gent for the naturall Love & affection which I now bear to EDWARD
LEWIS ye Younger Son of EDWARD LEWIS of TOTOSKEY CREEK in Rappa County
have granted & conferred & by these presents doth give & confirme unto ye sd EDWARD
LEWIS ye Younger his heirs & assignes forever all my right & title in two Cows marked
one of them with a swallow fork in the right ear with a nick under the sd Ear commonly known by ye name of Unicorne & the other marked with a crop in both ears & two
slits in each ear & underkeel in the right ear known by the name of Nancy & one
Yearling Cow Calfe together with all their Increase both male & female of the aforesd
Catle to ye sd EDWARD LEWIS the Younger his heirs & assignes for ever to have & to
hold the aforesd catle with all the Increase for evermore with warranty agt. me the sd
HUMPHRY BOOTH & my heirs & agt. all other persons claiming any right under them or
any of them. In Witness whereof I have hereunto set my hand & Seal this first day of

November Anno Domini 1665
in presence of SAMUEL GRIFFIN   HUMPHREY BOOTH   seal
    THOS. ℞ ROBINSON
Recognr. in Cur Com Rappa 2 die 9bris Ao. Dom 1665

pp.   KNOW ALL MEN by these presents that I JESPER GRIFFIN of Rappa. County Plan-
47-   ter do hereby for me my heirs Exrs. bargaine sell alienate & for ever set over
48   to ANTHONY GARRETT & JOHN SIBLY their heirs Exrs. & Admrs for ever one par-
    cell of land containing Three hundred acres lying situate upon RAPPA: CREEK
out of a Devident of Twelve hundred acres whereon I JESPER GRIFFIN now dwell the sd
Three hundred acres begining at a white Oak at the Eastern side of my Plantation & so
running according to ye usuall course till the three hundred acres be out which sd land
I doe hereby promise to acknowledge in Court when there to called & do bind my self
my heirs Exrs & admrs to defend the right of the sd land with all the priviledges & im-
munities thereto belonging to the sd ANTHONY & JOHN their heirs or assignes agt all
persons whatsoever. In Witness whereof I have hereunto set my hand & Seal this 2d
day of Novr. 1665
in presence of us SIMON℮₮ THOMAS   JESPER ✗ GRIFFIN seal
    JOHN⊬ HOWES
Recognr. in Cur Com Rappa 2 die 9bris 1665

pp.   KNOW ALL MEN by these presents that I JESPER GRIFFIN of the County of Rappa:
48-   Planter have sold unto WILLIAM TALBOTT of ye aforesaid County Planter one
49   parcell of land estimated about seventy acres of land being part of the aforesd
    GRIFFINs Devident now liveing upon now Know ye that I JESPER GRIFFIN do
bind me my heirs Exrs or assignes firmly by these presents that the aforesd WILLM.
TALBOTT his heirs or assignes shall enjoy the sd parcel of land without trouble or molestation of any person whatsoever with all priviledges of Planting Hunting Hawking
or fishing as the sd Land boundeth as followeth beginning on the North West side of ye
sd Plantation of the aforesaid GRIFFIN within ten paces of ye: fences & so runing to a
Chesnut upon the head of a branch marked runing down the South side of the Branch
into ye Swamp & so runing down the run unto the plantation side againe unto ye place
where it begineth for which sd land I the sd JESPER GRIFFIN do acknowledge to have
received full satisfaction & will acknowledge ye sd Sale in Court when required as Witness my hand & Seal the 23th July 1665
in presence of us THO: WHARTON   JESPER ᴹ GRIFFIN seal
    JOHN ⊥ ⱧHOWES (*Transcript HOWE)*
Recognr in Cur Com Rappa 2 die 9bris 1665

pp.   TO ALL TO WHOM &c. Now Know ye &c. that I the sd Sr. WILLIAM BERKLEY Knt &c
49-   with the consent of the Councell of State accordingly give & grant unto THOMAS
50   FRESHWATER 200 acres of land being on ye North side of RAPPA. RIVER upon a
    Creek called TOTOSKEY CREEK & on the water side of ye sd Creek & joynes to ye
land of LEONARD JONES & begineth at a marked Oak on ye sd: Creek side thence runing
for leanth into ye woods by a line of marked trees that devides this land from ye land of
ye sd JONES W. by S. unto a marked Spanish Oak by or nigh a branch that proceedeth out
of Mr. WILLIAMSONS CREEK thence No. by W. being its due breadth & the Course paral-
lel to the sd Creek side & finally thence down by & along the sd Creek side to the marked
tree where it begun the sd land being formerly granted unto ROBT. SISSON by Pattent
dated (blank) & by him deserted & upon petition of ye sd FRESHWATER it was granted

unto him ye 2d of ye Genll. Court held March last past by Order of ye Govr: & Councell to
have and to hold &c. to be held &c. yealding & paying &c. provided &c. Given at JAMES
CITY under my hand & the seal of the Colony this 30th of September 1664 Anoq Dom

THOMAS FRESHWATER his   WILLIAM BERKLEY
  Pattent for 300 acres of lande
Test FRA: KIRKMAN Cl Cur
Recordatr 10th 8ber 1665   Test PHILL LUDWELL Cl Off

pp.   THIS PRESENTS Witnesseth that I THOMAS FRESHWATER of ye County of Rappa:
50-   in Virga: for & in consideration of the sum of Fifteen hundred pounds of good
51   tobacco and Cask to me in hand paid by ROBT. SISSON of ye same County ye receipt whereof I do acknowledge have & do by these presents for my heirs Exrs: &
Admrs. Assigne over unto the sd ROBERT SISSON his heirs or assignes for ever the full
contents of this within mentioned Pattent with all & every the appurtenances therein
contained with warranty of the premises from any person or persons laying any lawfull claime to any of ye premises either from by or under me my heirs Exrs. Admrs. or
any of us. In Witness whereof I have hereunto set my hand & seal this 4th day of April
1664
in presence of us ABRAM COOMBE,   THOS. FRESHWATER   seal
      FRANCIS SUTLE
Recognr in Cur Com Rappa 2d 9bris 1665

pp.   TO ALL TRUE XPIAN PEOPLE to whom this present writeing shall come greeting
51-   Know ye that I NICHOLAS PEAD for & in consideration of Thirteen hundred &
52   Ninety pounds of good sound tobacco & caske already paid to me the sd NICHOLAS
      from ROBT. SISSON the receipt whereof I the sd NICHOLAS PEAD do hereby ack-
nowledge & thereof & of every part & parcell thereof doth hereby absolutely & freely
exonerate & by these presents discharge the sd ROBT. SISSON for ever have given
granted & confirmed & by these presents doth give sell & confirme unto the sd ROBERT
SISSON all my whole years Crop that is now hanging in ye House of ye sd ROBT. & also
one Cow called & known by the name of Rose marked with ye sign of a Popler Leaf to
have and to hold ye aforesaid Crop of Tobacco & Cow unto ye aforesaid ROBT. SISSON his
heirs & assignes for ever with Warranty agt me the sd NICHOLAS & all other persons
which may claime or pretend anything of a claime to the sd Crop by Deed Bargaines or
grants formerly made or granted. In Witness whereof I have hereunto set my hand &
Seal this 13th day of 8ber Ao. Dom 1665
in presence of us WILL. LLOYD   NICHOLAS |꜀꜀| BEADE
      JOHN ✗ FRANCE
Recognr in Cur Com Rappa 8 die Febry 1665

pp.   KNOW ALL MEN by these presents that I NICHOLAS BEADE of ye Parish of Farn-
52-   ham in ye County of Rappa:, Yeoman, have constituted ordained & appointed
53   & do by these presents constitute ordaine & appoint my trusty & welbeloved
      ffriend WILLIAM LOYD my true & lawfull attorny for me & in my name & for the
sole & better assurance of a certaine Deed of Bargaine & Sale made by me bearing date
with these presents unto ROBT. SISSON of ye Psh. of Farnham & County aforesaid Planter as by the sd Deed more at large it will appear & all & whatsoever my sd Attorny shall
do or cause to be done in the acknowledgement of ye said Deed according to Law & Act of
Assembly for the further & better assurance of the same unto the sd ROBT: SISSON I the
said NICHOLAS BEAD do acknowledge to be authentick firme & stable as if I my self were
personally present. In Witness whereof I have hereunto set my hand & seal this 30th

day of 8ber 1665
in presence of us JOHN I⌐2 SHERLOCK ye Elder   NICHOLAS ⋀⋀⋀ BEAD
   JOHN ⫙ SHERLOCK ye Younger
Recordatr: 12th 8br 1665 p RD Cl Cur

pp. BE IT KNOWN unto all men by these presents that I THOMAS BUTTON of the
53- County of Rappa: Planter do bestowe & give & by these presents make over one
54 firm Deed of Gift of Two hundred & nineteen acres three furlongs & Nineteen
   poles of land lying on ye South side of RAPPA: RIVER & in the sd County & on ye
Easterly side of a Branch of a Creek called Mr. YOUNGS CREEK & near the head of a
valley proceeding out of ye sd Branch Southerly & begineth at a marked red Oak unto
CHARLES GOODRICH Son of Lt. Coll: THOMAS GOODRICH of ye County aforesd. alienating
& Estrangeing from my self all my right title & interest in & of ye sd Land unto ye sd
CHARLES GOODRICH or his assignes for ever in as large & ample manner to have and to
hold the sd land as I am priviledged in ye Pattent thereunto belonging as witness my
hand & seal the 5th day of January in the year of our Lord 1663
Test RICHD: SILVESTER,   THOMAS BUTTON seal
  JOHN GATEWOOD
Recognr in Cur Com Rappa 6 die Febry 1665

pp. TO ALL TO WHOM &c. Now Know ye &c. that I the sd Sr. WILLIAM BERKLEY Knt:
54- Governour &c. do with the consent of the Councell of State accordingly give &
55 grant unto Mr. ALEX. FLEMING three hundred acres of land lying on the South
   side of RAPPA: RIVER in ye upper side of the Cod of the Bay opposite to a point
between NANSEMOND & NANSATIGMOND TOWN bounding & adjoying upon the North
West with CEDAR CREEK which devides this land & the land of JOHN GILLET North East
upon the River upon ye South East with another Creek & SW into the woods the sd Land
being formerly granted unto CLEMT. HERBERT by Pattent bearing date the 4th of Aprill
1657 & by him relinquished & upon petition of the sd Mr. FLEMING to the Governour &
Councell it was given & granted unto ye sd Mr. ALEX. FLEMING by an Order from the said
Governour & Councell bearing date the 28th March 1664 to have & to hold &c. to be held
&c. yealding & paying &c. provided &c. Given at JAMES CITY under my hand & the seal
of the Colony this 6th of Aprill 1664
        WILLIAM BERKLEY

 I ALEX. FLEMING do for & in consideration of a Sume of Tobacco to me in hand paid &
for divers considerations me thereunto moveing do by these presents acknowledge to
have bargained sold & firmly set to sale from me my heirs & assignes for ever ye within specified land containing Three hundred acres unto JAMES COGHILL his heirs &
assignes for ever & do bind me my heirs & assignes for ever to warrant the sd Sale from
any person claimeing from by or under me or from the Dower of my Wife ELIZA.
FLEMING & do promise to acknowledge the same in Court when thereunto lawfully
called & to the true performance hereof I hereunto set my hand & seal this 2d: day of
November Ao: 1664
in presence of us ENOCH DOUGHTY   ALEX. FLEMING seal
  ROBT. MAPES
Recognr in Cur Com Rappa 2 die 9bris 1665

p. I JAMES COGHILL do for & in consideration of a sum of Tobacco to be paid in hand
56 in consideration moveing do by these presents acknowledge to have bargained
  sold & firmly set to sale from me my heirs & assignes for ever the within speci-

fied land containing three hundred acres unto JOHN SPEED & his heirs & assignes for ever & do bind me my heirs & assignes for ever to warrant the sd Sale from any person claimeing from by or under me or from the Dower of my Wife ALICE COGHILL & do promise to acknowledge the same in Court when thereunto lawfully called & to the true performance hereof I have hereunto set my hand & seal this 19th day of 8ber 1665 in presence of us JOSEPH OKAINE,   JAMES COGHILL   seal
     ROBT. *M* GRINSIN, ARCHDALL COMBE
Recognr in Cur Com Rappa: 7 die febry 1665

pp.   KNOW ALL MEN by these presents that I ALICE COGHILL do make over unto JOHN
56-   SPEED my dower of the sd Three hundred acres of land which my husband have
57   sold to JOHN SPEED & to hold to him & his heirs for ever with all warranty &
        warrantyes that the Law requireth or may hereafter require from us & our
heirs for ever. In Witness whereof I have hereunto set my hand & seal Febry 5th 1665
     PETER CORNEWELL,   ALICE *A* COGHILL
     RICHARD STANFORD
Recordatr in Com Rappa: 12 die febry 1665 p RD Cl Cur

p.   I JOHN SPEED do for the consideration of a sum of tobacco in hand paid acknow-
57   ledged to have bargained & sold & do by these presents bargaine & sell from me
       & my heirs for ever the within specified land containing 300 acres unto THOMAS
FARREL his heirs & assignes for ever & do bind me & my heirs to Warrt: the sd Sale of Land from any person or persons claimeing by or under me. In Witness whereof I do hereunto set my hand & seal this 29th of May 1666
in presence of us JOHN CATLET,   JOHN*SI* SPEED   seal
     EDWARD ROUZEE
 This Deed of Sale abovementioned was by JOHN SPEED desired to be acknowledged in Court according to the intents above specified & thereupon to be recorded: May 29th 1666
Recognr: Coram Nobis   JOHN CATLET
                  THO: HAWKINS
Recognr: pr Colo. JOHN CATLET Capt: THOMAS HAWKINS 4 die July 1666
Recordatr: x die Test ROBT: DAVIS Cl Cur pred.

p.   KNOW ALL MEN by these presents that I MARY ALLEN do by virtue hereof con-
58   stitute make & ordaine JOHN SPEED my lawfull Attorny to acknowledge my Dower
      of One hundred & ten acres of land unto JAMES COGHILL from me my heirs unto
him & his heirs for ever. In Witness I have hereunto set my hand & seal February 5th 1665
     PETER CORNEWELL,   MARY *M* ALLEN   seal
     RICHARD STANFORD
Recognr: in Cur Com Rappa: 7 die febry 1665

pp.   KNOW ALL MEN by these presents that I THOMAS CHETWOOD in the County of
58-   LANC. in Virga: gent stand firmly bound & Obliged unto THOMAS WRIGHT of the
59   County of Rappa: , Mercht., in the sum of tenn thousand pounds of good tobacco
      & caske to be paid unto the sd THOMAS WRIGHT his heirs Exrs: Admrs: or assignes
conveniently in Rappa: County to the which paymt. well & truly to be made I bind me my heirs Exrs: & Admrs: firmely by these presents Sealed with my seal & dated this Seventh day of February 1665 &c
 Whereas the above bounden THOMAS CHETWOOD have sold & made sale of one thousand

acres of land to ye abovesaid THOMAS WRIGHT which sd Land lyeth in the Freshes of
RAPPA: RIVER & bounded according to the Pattent delivered by the said CHETWOOD to
the sd WRIGHT as relation thereunto had more at Large appeareth the Condition of this
Obligation is such yt. if the sd THOMAS WRIGHT his heirs & assigns shall & may from
time to time & at all times hereafter forever quietly & peacably hold occupy & enjoy the
land mentioned in the said Pattent with every part thereof in as large & ample manner
as is therein expressed without the hindrance or ejection of the said CHETWOOD his
heirs or assignes or any or either of them or any other persons whatsoever laying any
lawfull Right title or claime to the premises or any part thereof that then this present
Obligation to be void & of none effect or else to stand & remaine in full power force &
virtue

in presence of ALEX: FLEMING,   THO: CHETWOOD   seal
      WILLIAM LANE
Recognr: in Cur Com: Rappa 7 die febry 1665

pp.   THIS INDENTURE made the 27th day of December 1665 & in ye 17th: year of the
59-   Reign of our most gracious Sovereign Lord CHARLES the 2d: by the Grace of God
63   of England Scotland France & Ireland King defender of the faith &c. between
      JOHN MILLS of the County of Rappa. in Virga: Planter of the one part & THOMAS
POWELL of the same County Planter of the other part Witnesseth that the sd JOHN MILLS
as well for & in consideration of four hundred pounds of Merchantable tobacco & caske
& two Cows specified in a Bill of Sale made to the sd JOHN MILLS to him in hand by the
said THOMAS POWELL paid & delivered at or before the ensealing & delivery thereof the
said JOHN MILLS doth hereby acknowledge as also for the sd THOMAS POWELL is to
assure immediately upon the ensealing hereof unto the said JOHN MILLS his heirs &
assigns the aforesaid Cowes hath given granted sold & confirmed & by these presents
doth for him & his heirs give sell unto the said THOMAS POWELL his heirs & assignes
Fifty acres of land more or less begining & measuring from a marked Pocickery near
the MILL FLOODGATE bounding on ye: land of THOMAS ROOSON which is now possessed
by PHILLIP SAUNDERS & runneth for breadth by or near the Creek commonly called
TIGNERS CREEK unto a small run going into the sd Creek & so for leanth into the woods
to a marked white Oak near the sd Run lying on the West side of the now dwelling house
of the sd JOHN MILLS according to the Grand Pattent granted unto JOHN MILLS aforesaid
his heirs & assigns by the which ye aforesd Fifty acres of land is as mongst much more
held & enjoyed & all & singular the houseing buildings Orchards gardens Libertys of
fishing fowling hunting & all other proffits & hereditamts: whatsoever to ye sd Fifty
acres of land belonging or any wise appertaining thereof & the revertions & remain-
ders of the same premises or any part of them & all the Estate right of the sd JOHN
MILLS his heirs or assignes To have and to hold the said Fifty acres of land to the sd
THOMAS POWELL & his heirs & assignes with all the priviledges before mentioned to
the only use & behoof of the sd THOMAS POWELL his heirs & assignes for ever & the sd
JOHN MILLS for him & his heirs unto the said THOMAS POWELL his heirs & assignes
shall & will for ever Warrt: & defend by these presents & the said JOHN MILLS for his
heirs & for every of them doth grant with the sd THOMAS POWELL his heirs & assignes
by these presents (Vizt:) that the sd JOHN MILLS & JOANE his Wife shall & will before
the end of six months next ensuing the date hereof before the Worshipfull his Matys
Justices of the peace for the County of Rappa: aforesd at the Court holden for the said
County personally appear or by their Lawfull Attorny & then & there acknowledge all
& singular the right & interest of ye premises aforesd to be vested in the sd THOS.
POWELL & it is the true meaning of all the sd persons that the said acknowledgemt. shall
be taken for & as a fine Sur Cognizance &c with proclamations thereupon according to

the Statutes of England in that case made & provided & further that the said JOHN MILLS
& his heirs & all others claimeing under him will at all times hereafter during the
space of five years next ensuing date hereof at the reasonable request proper costs &
Charges in the Law of the sd THOMAS POWELL his heirs & assignes make all such re-
leases & conveyances in the Law unto the said THOMAS POWELL his heirs & assignes or
by his or their Learned Councell in the Law shall be reasonably required so as the person so required be not compelled to go out of the Country of Virga: & it is agreed by the
sd partyes by these presents that such further or other assurancy shall be taken &
deemed to be for the proper use & behoof of the sd THOMAS POWELL his heirs & assignes
alwayes provided the sd THOMAS his heirs & assignes shall pay the Quitrents due to his
Majesty unto JOHN MILLS his heirs or assignes when the same shall be required. In
Witness whereof the said JOHN MILLS to this present Indenture hath set his hand & seal
the day & year first above written
in presence of us JOHN NOBLE,   JOHN M MILLS   seale
        ROBT. GOODYEAR

p.   KNOW ALL MEN by these presents that I JOANE MILLS the now Wife of JOHN
63   MILLS of ye County of Rappa: in Virga: do hereby constitute & appoint my
        Loving Friend THOMAS ROOSON my true & lawfull attorny in my name & steed to
acknowledge my full & free consent to the Sale of a peice of Land unto THOMAS POWELL
as is expressed in a Conveyance made to yt: purpose & I do hereby confirme & rattify
what my said Attorny shall do therein to be as good in Law as if I my self had in person
done the same as witness my hand & seal this 5th: day of February 1665
in presence of REBECCA + GOODRIG   JOANE I MILLS   seale
        JOHN X GOODRIG
Recognr in Cur Com Rappa: 7 die febry 1665 Record 12th

p.   TO ALL TO WHOM &c. Now Know ye &c that I the said Sr. WILLIAM BERKLEY Knt.
64   Governour & Capt. Generall of Virga: &c. do with the consent of ye Counsel of
        State accordingly give and grant unto JOHN HULL three hundred acres of land
lying in LANC. COUNTY upon OCCUPATION CREEK & begining at a white Oak upon a
branch proceeding from the sd Creek extending it self parrallel thereunto NE unto a
nother branch into the woods a mile SE afterwoods the aforesaid Courses opposite for-
ming a Quadrangle the sd land being formerly granted JOHN WATSON by Pattent dated
the 12th of June 1655 & by him sold unto VINCT: STANFORD & by STANFORD sold unto
EDWARD HUDSON & by the sd HUDSON sold & assigned to the sd JOHN HULL to have and to
hold &c. to be held &c yealding & paying &c provided &c Given under my hand at
JAMES CITY the Seal of the Colony this 18th of March 1662 &c
Recordatr 27th Aprill 1665   WILLIAM BERKLEY
        Test PHILL LUDWELL Cl Off

pp.   KNOW ALL MEN by these presents that I within named JOHN HULL for & in con-
64-   sideration of Four thousand pounds of Tobo: at ye Sealing & delivery hereof by
65   WILL. SPICER, Carpentr., well & truly paid the receipt whereof I doe hereby
        acknowledge & throughly clearly acquit & discharge the sd WILL SPICER his
Exrs. Admrs or assignes have granted sold & confirmed & by these presents do for me
my heirs & assignes fully & absolutely grant sell & confirme unto ye sd WILLM. SPICER
his heirs & assignes all & singular that three hundred acres of land within mentioned
with all rights & proffits belonging to the same & also all my right & interest of the
same to have & to hold the sd Three hundred acres with all his rights & proffits of the
same he the sd SPICER paying all rights due for the same unto the sd WILLM. SPICER

his heirs & assignes for ever. In Witness hereof I have set my hand & seale this 7th: of
February Ao. Dom, 1665
in presence of us THO. GOODRICH,   JOHN HULL   seale
     W. MOSELEY
Recognr in Cur Com Rappa 7 die febry 1665   ROBERT DAVIS Cl Cur

pp.   Februay the 7th: 1665. RECEIVED then of Mr. RICHARD LAWRENCE full satisfac-
65-   tion from all Debts dues & demands whatsoever from him to Mr. RICHARD
66   KNIGHT of BOSTON in NEW ENGLAND & in particular from a Bill of Thirteen hun-
      dred & twelve pounds of tobacco & caske or thereabouts as witness my hand the
day & year abovesaid I being the Attorny of the said KNIGHT
                                     THO. HAWKINS
Recognr: in Cur Com Rappa 7 die february 1665

p.   I JOHN MILLS do give unto my Daughter ELIZA: MILLS one Cow named Crow & all
66   her increase both male & female which Cow is marked with a crop & an under-
      keel in the right ear in the left ear a crop & two slits in the crop & all her in-
crease I give to the sd ELIZA: & her heirs as witness my hand this 7th of February 1665
                                  JOHN ₩ MILLS
Recognr: in Cur Com Rappa 7 die febry 1665

pp.   KNOW ALL MEN by these presents that I THOMAS GOODRICH of the County of
66-   Rappa: do here give grant & deliver unto JANE BUTTON to her own proper use
67   one Cow calfe with her increase that is not marked of the Stock of MICHAEL
      BARON for her Care & Paines in preserving ye sd Catle I being an Attorny for
the said BARON & do hereby these presents give grant & confirme this Cow calf unto
JANE BUTTON her heirs for ever from any person or persons whatsoever that shall lay
any claime to the said Calfe in as firme & ample manner as if MICHAEL BARON were
here himself present as witness my hand 18th May 1664
Test ANTHONY WATTS,   THO: GOODRICH
     ELATHY ⨎ ELTHERSON the marke of
Recognr: in Cur Com Rappa 7 die february 1665

p   I RICHARD LAWRENCE do by these presents assigne over all my right & title unto
67   a Servant made named REBECCA SUMMERLAND unto MICHAEL HUGELL or as-
      signes for the full terme that she hath to serve by Custom or otherwise she
comeing into this Country without Indentures in the Ship whereof JUNIFER PLOWER
was Commander in the year of our Lord 1662. As Witness my hand this 17th: day of
febry 1664
in presence of us WALTER SIMMS,   RICHARD LAWRENCE seal
     KATHERINE ✗ SIMMS her marke
Recognr: in Cur Com Rappa 7 die febry 1665

p.   KNOW ALL MEN by these presents that I ROBT: MUSSELL of the County of Rappa:
68   Planter doe for the good will I bear to my Friend RICHARD TAYLOR of the same
      County to place constitute and appoint the sd TAYLOR to be my Genl. Attorny to
sue implead or to answer to any Suit of Law depending concerning me in the County
Court or to acknowledge Judgmt: if occasion shall be & to give acquittance in my name
also as powerfull as if I my self were there present in person. Given under my hand
this 6th day of February 1665

in presence of us WILL HODGKINS,   ROBT. R M MUSSELL
        HUGH EGELSTON
Recordatr 12 die febry 1665

pp.   KNOW ALL MEN by these presents that I MARY FANTLEROY have made consti-
68-   tuted & appointed & by these presents do make constitute & depute WILLIAM
69   LOYD to be my true & lawfull attorny for me & in my name to prosecute or de-
        fend any action or actions which shall be brought in my name or to defend any
action whatsoever that shall be brot: agt: me the said MARY FANTLEROY & whatsoever
my sd Attorny shall do or cause to be done in the abovesd premises I the sd MARY
FANTLEROY do hereby rattify & confirme & allow of as amply & fully as if I myself were
personally present. In Witness whereof I the said MARY FANTLEROY have hereunto set
my hand & seal this 6th of February Ao: Dom: 1665
Witnesses hereunto
    the marke of M MARY BEACHAM   MARY FANTLEROY   seal
    the marke of F W JOHN WOOD
Recordatr 12 febry 1665

pp.   November the 3th: 1665
69-   Dr. DAVIS I formerly writ to you per Capt: HAWKINS to appear as my Attorny &
70   now againe desire the same favour I have desired Mr: HAWKINS to give you the
        Bill of Capt: BRYERS which pray procure an order of Court agt GOOSE & also de-
mand of the condition of this HUGH DANIEL who hath arrested me for worke done in
part & I him as pr: my petition will appear then may be please to write a Shorter petition & make use of the rest to plead or what you think most Convenient I leave it to
your discretion which pray manage with what care you can for yor:
                                friend & Servt.
                                        THO: BOWLER
    Pray take the order from the Clerk that was passed Six months agoe agt: one BARBER
yt: Marryed ye: Relict of JOHN TARPLEY & take Execution on it & send it me with the rest
of your proceedings by Mr. CORBYN or by the first opportunity
    Recordatr in Com Rappa 12 die Feb 1665   p RD Cl Cur

p.   These are to Authorize my loving Friend Mr. RICHARD WEBLY my true & lawfull
70   Attorny to act & doe in a bussiness depending in this Court between me & JOHN
        BARROW & him to implead & discharge & acquit as if I my self were there pre-
sent witness my this 7th: March 1665
Test HUM: BOOTH   W. MOSELEY
Recorded the 10th day of March 1665/6
                Test ROBT. DAVIS Cl Cur

pp.   KNOW ALL MEN by these presents that I RICHARD LAWRENCE of the County of
70-   Rappa: do hereby acknowledge & confess that I have bargained for & sold unto
71   ROBT: HILL of the County of LANC. his heirs & assignes three hundred acres of
        land that part of the within mentioned Patt: belonging unto me RICHARD
LAWRENCE for a valluable consideration to my own content already in hand reced of
the abovesd ROBT. HILL his heirs & assignes to which Land aforesd with all rights &
priviledges thereunto belonging I the sd RICHARD LAWRENCE do acknowledge & oblige
my self my heirs & assignes unto ROBT. HILL his heirs & assignes for the Quiet & peace-
able enjoymt: of the sd Land from any person whatsoever that shall lay claime to the
same further I do hereby bind my self my heirs to make good the sale of the said land &

to keep him the said ROBT: HILL his heirs & assignes harmless & indemnified from all
manner or molesltation whatseover from any persons that shall hereafter lay claime
unto the said land or any part thereof in the penalty of the paymt: of Six thousand
pounds of good Virga. tobacco & caske unto him the sd ROBT. HILL his heirs or assignes
to this my act & deed I have set my hand & seal this 7th March 1665
in presence of us JOHN RYMAN,   RICHARD LAWRENCE seal
        THO: PATTISON
Recognr: in Cur Com Rappa 7 die Martii Ao. 1665

p.   The Marke of the Catle & Hoggs of FRANCIS SETLE is Vizt. the right ear cropt &
72   the left ear an under keel & a slit down the Ear
        Recordatr: x die Martii Ao. 1665

pp.   TO ALL XPIAN PEOPLE to whom these presents shall come We ROBT: SISSON &
72-   QUINTILLIAN SHEREMAN for a valluable consideration have given sold & con-
73   firmed unto ANDREW HERBERT all our Estate right & interest of one Plantation
        lately sold by Mr. BOOTH unto the afd. ROBT. SISSON known by the name of the
OLD PLANTATION Cont. by estimation three hundred acres be it more or less now in the
possession of the said ANDREW HERBERT to have & to hold ye aforesaid plantation with
all rights & priviledges whatsoever together with their & every of their appurtenances
unto the sd ANDREW HERBERT his heirs & assignes for ever with warranty agt: me the
said ROBT: SISSON & the sd QUINTILLIAN SHEREMAN our & either of our heirs & assignes
& further the sd ROBT: SISSON & QUINTILLIAN SHEREMAN covenants & granteth to &
with the sd ANDREW HERBERT his heirs & assignes upon demand at any time of one
whole year from the date hereof make further assurance or conveyance of the aforesaid premises for the further and better perfecting and assuring of the sd primises &
Lastly the sd ROBT: SISSON hereby promiseth to cause his now Wife AMYE SISSON to
make or cause to be made an acknowledgemt. at the next Court of all her right title
thirds or Dower of the aforesaid premises. In Witness whereof we have hereunto set
our hands & seals this 7th day of March Ao. Dom 1665
Witnesses hereunto THO: GOOSE,   ROBT: SISSON   seal
        WILL LOYD   (No signature for Sherman)
Recognr: in Cur Com: Rappa 7 die Martii Ao. 1665

pp.   KNOW ALL MEN by these presents that I SAML: GRIFFIN of the County of Rappa:
73-   Mercht., for divers good considerations & causes me thereunto moving do here-
74   by give & grant unto THOMAS GRIFFIN Son of THOS: GRIFFIN deced a young Mare
        of a Dun Coulour with a white Starr in her forehead to have & to hold ye sd Mare
with all her increase (except the males) unto him ye sd THOMAS GRIFFIN & his heirs for
ever in Testimony whereof I have hereunto set my hand & seal this 6th day of March
Ao. Dom: 1665
Witness JOHN HULL,   SAM. GRIFFIN   seal
        THO: HAWKINS
Recognr: in Cur Com: Rappa: 7 die Martii 1665:6
                Test ROBT. DAVIS Cl Cur

pp.   KNOW ALL MEN by these presents that I RICHARD JONES of the County of LOWER
74-   NORFOLK in ELIZA: RIVER for & in consideration of Eight thousand pounds of
75   good tobacco & caske by Bill secured of THO: PAGE, RICHD: WEST & SAML.
        WELLDING of the County of Rappa: have given granted sold & confirmed & do
by these presents give bargaine sell & confirme unto the said THO: PAGE, RICHARD WEST

& SAMUEL WELDING all my right & title & interest of in & to the one halfe of a Devident of land as is specified in a Pattent bearing date the 20 day of February in the year of our Lord 1662 cont. by the Pattent Six hundred acres of land bounding to ye East upon JOHN WATSON & from thence runing West upon the River 300 poles & bounding thereupon Mr. THOMAS LUCAS SENR. & from the River a Mile backwards into the woods the East part of which said Land with the Clear ground & all the houses & edifices thereunto appertaining & belonging & all & every of the aforesd premises I do sell & make over from me the sd RICHARD JONES my heirs & admrs. to the sd THO. PAGE, RICHD. WEST & SAML. WELDING their heirs & assignes in as large & ample manner to all intents & purposes as the sd MOSELEYs or half part was formerly sold & conveyed to me from the sd THOMAS PAIGE by Conveyance bearing date the 28 day of October 1664. In Witness whereof I have hereunto set my hand & seal this 6th day of March 1665

in presence of us   JOHN WEIR   RICHD.   JONES   seal

          ROBT. DAVIS

Recognr in Cur Com Rappa 7 die Martii Ao: 1665

pp.   KNOW ALL MEN by these presents that we THOMAS PAIGE & RICHARD WEST both
75-   of the County of Rappa: in Virga: stand firmly bound & indebted unto RICHD.
76   JONES of the County of LOWER NORFOLK in ELIZA. RIVER in the sum of Nine

thousand three hundred fifty and two pounds of Tobo: & Caske to be paid to the sd JONES his heirs or assignes to the which paymt: well & truly to be made we bind us either & every of us our heirs firmly by these presents sealed with our seals & dated this sixth day of March 1665 &c

THE CONDITION of this obligation is such yt: if the above bounden THO: PAIGE & RICHARD WEST or either of them their or either of their heirs or assignes shall well & truly pay unto the sd RICHARD JONES his heirs or assignes the just sum of Four thousand Six hund: Seventy & six pounds of good sound bright & large tobacco clear of trash ground leaves & Seconds with Sufft: Caske conveniently in Rappa: County & in the Parish of Sittenbourne at or upon the tenth day of October next ensuing the day of the date hereof that then this present obligiation to be void & of none effect or else to stand & remaine in full power force & virtue

in presence of us   JOHN WEIR.   THO: P PAIGE   seal

          ROBT. DAVIS   RICHD: ꝶ WEST   seal

Recognr in Cur Com Rappa: 7 die Martii 1665

pp.   WHEREAS the difference depending Between Mr. FRANCIS DOUGHTY and SILVES-
76-   TER THATCHER is put to the Arbitracion of us under Subscribing both by the
77   consent of the parties and Order of Court and the difference depending being

about the Charge and Expence for a Quarter part of the good BARQUE called the *RETURNE* it doth appear unto us by the Evidence of Mr. ALEXR: FLEMING, Capt. JOHN WEIRE and Mr. WILLIAM MOSELEY that the part the said SILVESTER THATCHER was interested and possessed of was sold unto JOHN HINKSMAN & KENELINE WINSLOW and accepted of by their Attorney Mr. THOMAS HAWKINS with both the profit and loss of the voyages made while the sd THATCHER was Owner.

We do award Mr. FRANCIS DOUGHTY his Remedy of his Charges and expences against JOHN HINKSMAN and KENELINE WINSLOE and do clear SILVESTER THATCHER of those charges as we do attest this 3d of March 1664

                              THO. GOODRICH

                              WILLM. HALL

                              WILLIAM LANE

Recordatr. x die   JOHN STONE

pp.   TO ALL TO WHOM &c Now Know ye &c that I the said Sr. WILLIAM BERKLEY Knt:
77-   &c do with the consent of the Councell of State accordingly give and grant unto
78   Mr. THOMAS PADDISON & Mr. WILLIAM DENBY five hundred & four acres of land
        lying in the County of Rappa: upon the South side of RAPPA: parte thereof lying
by the river side & parte upon the back line of Mr. THOMAS PAINE & Mr. JAMES BAG-
NALL deced & bounded as following Vizt: begining at Mr: TOBIAS SMITHs lower Corner
tree by the River being a red Oak standing nigh the Rivers bank & runing Wt. S. Wt.
inclining Southerly 320 poles along the land of the sd SMITH thence S. Wt. 100 poles by
marked trees backing the land of Mr. PAINE aforesd SSE 294 poles to a Spanish Oak corner by a branch side thence 36 poles to a corner white Oak standing by a forked Chesnut SSE alonge the land of JOHN SHARPE parte thereof to a corner Oak standing in
SHARPEs line thence N. by Wt. Northerly to ye land of Mr. JAMES BAGNALL & alonge his
back lyne No: No: Wt: to Mr. PAINEs lande back lyne & alonge his line to the Westermost
Corner thereof & down his line to the River NE & up the River 17 poles to the Corner
tree it first began To have & to hold &c to be held &c Yealding & paying &c Provided &c
Given at JAMES CITY under my hand & the Seal of the Colony this 3 day of December
1663 & in the 15th year of the Reign of our Sovereign Lord KING CHARLES the Second
&c
THOMAS PADDISON & WM. DENBY   WILLIAM BERKLEY
  Patt. for 504 acres of land
                          Test FRA: KIRKMAN

p.   Witness these presents that wee THOMAS PADDISON & my Wife ANN PADDISON do
79   assigne all our right & title from us our heirs Exrs. or assignes unto THOMAS
        BOWLER his heirs Executors or Assignes for Ever the one just half of land that is
conteyned in this patten more or less as Witness our hands this 25th of Febry 1664
Test WILL: HODGKINS,   THOMAS PATTISON
     THO: HARWAR   ANN PATTISON
Recognr: in Cur Com Rappa: 2 die Martii Ao. 1664

pp.   THIS INDENTURE made this 14th day of February 1664 Between THOMAS PATTISON
79-   of the County of Rappa: in Virga: Planter & THOMAS BOWLER, Mercht., of the sd
81   County Witnesseth that said THOMAS PATTISON for & in consideration of a vallu-
        able consideration reced to him at or before the ensealing & delivery of these
presents & truly in hand paid by the sd THOMAS BOWLER whereof & wherewith he the
said THOMAS PATTISON doth acknowledge himself well contended have granted sold &
confirmed by these presents doth fully & absolutely grant & set over unto the said THO-
MAS BOWLER his heirs or assignes for ever all that messuage of land as is by Pattent
confirmed unto me situate & being in the Parish of Farnham in the County of Rappa: as
aforesaid To have & to hold the sd Messuage of land containing by estimation as by Pattent will appear 252 acres it being the one half of five hundred & four acres betwixt
WILLIAM DENBY & the said THOMAS PATTISON as by the said Pattent doth make appear
be it more or less that was taken up by the said PATTISON & every parte thereof from
henceforth & to continue to the sd THOMAS BOWLER his heirs or assignes for ever & do
hereby warrt: against all men all & every part of the said Land & all things whatsoever
thereupon the sd Land the said THOMAS BOWLER his heirs or assignes quietly to enjoy
for ever from all former bargaines suites gifts grants dowers leases charges or rent
uses judgments forfeitures or executions intrusions or incumbrances whatsoever & the
sd THOMAS PATTISON his heirs or assignes shall at all times hereafter within the space
of five years next ensuing at the request of sd THOMAS BOWLER his heirs acknowledge
every article or assurances in the Land whatsoever to the further assurance of all ye

premises abovemenconed in the full Sale of the said Land & all whatsoever belonging
unto sd THOMAS BOWLER his heirs & assignes for ever as he or his Councell in the Law
Learned shall devise or require as witness my hand & seal this 25th day of February
1664

in presence of us WILL HODGKINS,   THO. PATTISON   seal
          THO: HARWAR

Recognr. in Cur Com Rappa: 2d die Martii Ao. 1664

pp.   KNOW ALL MEN by these presents that I THOMAS PATTISON of Rappa: in Virga:
81-   Planter am hereby firmly held & stand indebted unto THOMAS BOWLER Mercht.
82   of the same County the sum of Two thousand four hundred pounds of tobacco
         to be paid to sd THOMAS BOWLER his heirs or assignes to which payment truly to
be made I bind me my heirs & admrs. firmly by these presents sealed with my seal &
dated this 25th day of February 1664/5

  THE CONDITION of this obligation is such yt: if the within named THOMAS BOWLER his
heirs or assignes & every of them shall & may forever from henceforth peacably &
quietly have use possess & enjoy all that messuage & Lands situate lying & being in the
Parish of Farnham & County of Rappa: & every part & parcell thereof mentioned to be
sold by the within bound THOMAS PATTISON to the aforesaid THOMAS BOWLER in & by a
certaine Indenture of Bargaine & Sale bearing date the twenty fifth day of February
made between the within bound THOMAS PATTISON on the one pt: & the abovenamed
THOMAS BOWLER on the other parte clearly discharged or otherwise suffly saved & kept
harmless from all manner of Estates titles troubles & incumbrances whatsoever at any
time heretofore committed or done by the said THOMAS PATTISON or by his or any
others procuremt: that then this present obligation to be void & of none effect Otherwise to stand & remaine in full power & Virtue as witness my hand & Seal this twenty
fifth day of February 1664

in presence of us WILL HODGKINS,   THO. PATTISON   seal
          THO. HARWAR

Recognr. in Cur Com: Rappa: 2 die Martii Ao. 1664

pp.   We THOMAS PATTISON & my Wife ANN PATTISON doth constitute & appoint Mr.
82-   THOMAS HARWAR our lawfull Attorny for the acknowledging of our right &
83   title from us our heirs or assignes for ever in the one half of a piece of land as
         by Pattent will appear with our hands to it for the assignmt: & also the sd HAR-
WAR to acknowledge the Bill of Sale & Bond of it for the use of THOMAS BOWLER his
heirs or assignes for ever as Witness our hands this 25th day of February 1664
          WILL HODGKINS,   THO. PATTISON
          JOHN SEARGANT   ANN PATTISON

Recordatr: x die Martii Ao. 1664 p ROBERT DAVIES Cl Cur

pp.   KNOW ALL MEN by these presents that I THOMAS BROWNE of the County of
83-   ACCOMACK in Virga: for divers considerations me hereunto especially moveing
84   & for & in consideration of Two Servants to me to be paid as is expressed by two
         Bills bearing date with these presents do hereby give & grant all my right title
& interest of a Pattent of Six hundred & sixty acres of land formerly WILLIAM YARRITs
& sold by the said WILLIAM YARRIT to Mr. SMART & assigned to my Loving Mother
URSULA BROWN alias FLEMING as by ye sd Assignemt: may appear. Now Know ye that I
THOMAS BROWN do deliver up all my right of the sd Land from me & my heirs unto my
Father in Law Capt. ALEX: FLEMING & his heirs & assignes for ever with all appurtenances belonging to the said Land from me & my heirs In Witness to the abovesaid

premises I hereunto set my hand & Seal this 14th day of February Ao. 1664
in presence of ROBT: MAPES,   THOMAS BROWN   seal
         JOHN GAINES

pp.   I THOMAS BROWN of the County of ACCOMACK in Virginia do by these presents
84-   constitute & appoint my Loveing Friend ROBERT MAPES my true & lawfull Attor-
85   ney for me & in the behalf of me & my heirs to acknowledge a Pattent or an
         assignmt: of Six hundred & Sixty acres of land that I the said THOMAS BROWN
have given & granted unto my Father in Law Capt. ALEXANDER FLEMING & his heirs
the said land being formerly Mr. WILLIAM YARRETTs & from him assigned to SMART &
so from Mr. WILLIAM SMART sold to my Loving Mother Mrs: URSULA BROWN alias
FLEMING I give power to my sd Attorny to acknowledge the sd Land in the County Court
according to Law & whatsoever my attorny shall do in the premises I shall allow.
In witness whereof I hereunto set my hand & seal this 14th day of February 1664
Test WILL HOGGE.   THO. BROWNE   seal
     THO. SNEDE
Recognr. in Cur Com Rappa: 3 die Martii Ao. 1664

pp.   TO ALL XPIAN PEOPLE to whom these presents shall come Know Ye that wee JOHN
85-   SHARPE by & with the Consent of JUDITH my Wife & HENRY CREIGHTON by &
86   with the consent of FRANCIS my Wife for divers good causes & valuable con-
         siderations us thereunto moving & more especially for the sume of Four thou-
sand Five hundred pounds of good tobacco & Caske to us in hand paide by JOHN PAINE of
the County of Rappa: which wee acknowledge to have received have given sold & confirmed & do by these presents give sell & confirme unto the said JOHN PAINE all that
parcell & divident of land which we bought of WILLIAM SAVADGE & WILLIAM LIN-
NELL begining at a white Oake marked upon the Edge of the Swampe & so runing West
South West unto an INDIAN PATH & from thence to the same Swamp where we first
began the sd Land being formerly sold by the said PAINE to ye: said SAVADGE, ROBT:
MUSSELL & WILLIAM LINNEL to have and to hold the said Divident of land with every
part & parcell thereof with all rights & priviledges to him the sd JOHN PAINE his heirs
& assignes for ever the said JOHN PAINE his heirs or assignes yeilding & paying from
henceforth yearly his Matys Rights dues & accustomed for the same & we the said JOHN
SHARPE & JUDITH my Wife & HENRY CREIGHTON & FRANCIS my Wife do hereby promise
& grant to & with the said JOHN PAINE his heirs & assignes that he & they shall at all
times hereafter quietly enjoy the abovementioned premises with every part & parcell
thereof without the hindrances or interruption of us or either or any of our heirs or
assignes or any other persons whatsoever claimeing the aforementioned premises or
any part thereof by or under us our or any of our heirs or assignes. In Witness
whereof we have hereunto set our hands & seals this 26th day of April 1665
in presence of us JOHN FENNELL, A   JOHN ☉ SHARPE   seal
        JOHN SHATFORD,   JUDITH I SHARPE   seal
        ELIAS X WILSON   HENRY CREIGHTON   seal
                                                     FRANCES CREIGHTON   seal

pp.   KNOW ALL MEN by these presents that I JUDITH SHARPE of ye County of Rappa:
86-   doth constitute & appoint my Loving Friend JOHN NEWMAN to be my lawfull
87   Attorny for me & in my steed to acknowledge a tract of land sold by my Husband
         unto JOHN PAINE. In Witness whereof I have hereunto set my hand this 28th:
day of Aprill 1665

Test   HENRY CREIGHTON   JUDITH I SHARPE
        JOHN SHATFORD

p.   KNOW ALL MEN by these presents that I FRANCES CREIGHTON do constitute & ap-
87   point my Loveing Friend Mr. RICHARD WEBLEY for me & in my steed to acknow-
        ledge one parcell of land sould by HENRY CREIGHTON my Husband unto JOHN
PAINE as Witness my hand this 2 of May 1665
Test ELIAS x WILSON,   FRANCES CREIGHTON
     THOMAS 0 NEWMAN
Recognr: in Cur Com Rappa: 4 die May 1665

pp.   KNOW ALL MEN by these presents that I LUKE BILLINGTON of the County of
87-   Rappa: Plantr: for & in consideration of good & real Satisfaction to me in hand
89   paid & delivered by DENNIS SILLIVANT of the County aforesaid have granted sold
        & confirmed & by these presents doth sell & confirme unto the sd DENNIS
SILLIVANT his heirs or assignes for ever One hundred Eighty & six acres of land situate
& being upon RICHARDS CREEK & in the County of Rappa: aforesaid where he the aforesd SILLIVANT now Liveth & bounding upon the land of Mr: ROBT. BAILIST & JAMES
SAMPFORD, JOHN CANADEE & Mr: WEBB this land being part of a devident of land cont.
252 acres of land & formerly purchased by LUKE BILLINGTON of Colo: MOOR FANTLEROY
the aforesaid SILLIVANT to have & to hold ye sd one hundred Eighty & six acres of land
with the appurtenances unto the sd DENNIS SILLIVANT his heirs or assignes for ever
the said DENNIS SILLIVANT his heirs or assignes yealding paying doing discharging
performing the rents & services due & payable for the same & I the said LUKE BILLING-
TON for me my heirs do by these presents agree to & with the said DENNIS SILLIVANT
his heirs or assignes that said DENNIS SILLIVANT shall or lawfully may at all times
hereafter forever quietly enjoy the said premises by these presents granted without
the Incumbrance of me the said LUKE BILLINGTON my heirs or assignes or any other
persons whatsoever lawfully claimeing the sd premises or any parte thereof. In Witness whereof I the sd LUKE BILLINGTON have hereunto set my hand & seal this 2d: day
of February 1663
in presence of us JOHN POTTER   LUKE BILLINGTON   seal
      WILL BARBER   BARBARY B BILLINGTON   seal
Recognr: in Cur Com Rappa 4 die Janry 1663

pp.   KNOW ALL MEN by these presents that I DENNIS SILLIVANT of the County of
89-   Rappa: do with the consent of JOHANNA my Wife assigne transfer & make over
90   from my my heirs Exrs: Admrs: or assignes the within mentioned Conveyance &
        land therein expressed unto TOBIAS STEVENS & WM. KENNY their heirs Exrs: or
assignes for ever. In Witness of the same I have hereunto set my hand & seal this 28th
day of October Ao. Dom 1664
Test SAM. DENNETT   DENNIS E SILLIVANT   seal
     AYLIS CANDSLOW   JOHANNA f SILLIVANT   seal

    KNOW ALL MEN by these presents that I JOANE SWELLIVANT Wife of DENNIS SWILLI-
VANT of the County of Rappa. do put & constitute THOMAS FRESHWATER to be my true &
lawfull Attorney for me & in my name & steed to acknowledge a parcell of land sold by
my abovesaid Husband unto TOBY STEVENS & WILLIAM KENNY of the said County giving
& granting unto my said Attorny as full power in & abt. the premises as if I myself were
personally present & for the true performance of the same I have hereunto set my
hand & seal this last day of Decr: 1664

Testis JAMES WEBB,   JOANE X SWELLIVANT   seal
        SAML. PEACHY
Recognr. in Cur Com Rappa 5 die Janry Ao. 1664

pp.   KNOW ALL MEN by these presents that I RICHD. WEST of the Parish of Sitting-
90-   bourne in the County of Rappa. have for a valluable consideration by me in
91   hand reced bargained & sold and do by these presents bargaine sell and make
        over unto JOHN BURKY of the place aforesaid the half part of a parcell of land to
me belonging formerly Pattent by me & ROGER CLOTWORTHY bearing date July the 28th
1663 the said land being already devided between us the sd RICHARD WEST & JOHN
BURKY by mutual consent by a line of marked trees begining at a marked red Oak
standing near the clear ground of ROGER CLOTWORTHY & so across the aforesaid land
the Eastermost part of which land adjoyning to a branch commonly called POPOMANS
BRANCH I the said RICHARD WEST do as aforesaid make over the aforesd land to the afd.
JOHN BURKY from me my heirs Exrs. Admrs. or assignes to him his heirs Exrs. Admrs. or
assignes for ever to the truth whereof Witness my hand & Seal this 3d: of Janry 1664
in presence of THO: HAWKINS,   RICHARD R WEST   seal
        ALICE C FULLER

p.   I RICHARD WEST do hereby constitute & appoint my loving Friend THOMAS HAW-
91   KINS my true & lawfull attorny for me & in my name to acknowledge the sale of
        a parcell of land unto JOHN BURKY or his Order in Court & what my attorny shall
do in ye premises I do hereby promise to confirme & allow to the truth whereof witness
my hand this 3d: of January 1664
Witness ALICE O FULLER,   RICHARD R WEST   seal
        THO. X MELTON
Recognr. in Cur Com Rappa 5 die January 1664

pp.   KNOW ALL MEN by these presents that I THOMAS WILLIAMSON & EVAN DAVIS
91-   both of the County of Rappa: Plantrs: do acknowledge & confess that we joyntly
93   have bargained for & sould unto PETER BAWCOMB of the County aforesaid his
        heirs Exrs. Admrs. & assignes Six hundred acres of land more or less for a vallu-
able consideration to our own contentment already in hand reced the sd Land being
their sevel: parts of a tract of land Pattented in the name of RICHARD LAWRENCE & the
sd THOS. WILLIAMSON & EVAN DAVIS containing Nine hundred acres lying & being on
the South side of RAPPA RIVER & in Rappa County begining at a marked white Oak
standing on the Eastermost side of a WHITE MARSH at the head of a branch issuing out
of ye DRAGON SWAMP & crossing MATTAPONY UPPER PATH thence runing Southerly
along the said Branch to the DRAGON SWAMP then Easterly along the sd Swamp to
another branch thereof thence alongst the Path 24 degrees North West thence West &
by North 204 poles to the first specified place the which land with all rights & priviledges thereunto belonging we the sd THOMAS WILLIAMSON & EVAN DAVIS do acknowledge & into the possession deliver unto him the sd PETER BAWCOMB his heirs or assignes for ever to be by him & them quietly enjoyed & possessed & we do further for
ever quit all claime title or interest to the sd land or any part thereof from us the said
THOS. WILLIAMSON & EVAN DAVIS our heirs or assignes forever to this our act & deed to
be placed in the publick Records according to Law thereunto provided We hereunto set
our hands & seals this 20th day of April 1664
in presence of THO. PATTYSON,   THO. T WILLIAMSON   seal
        ROGER R G GREEN   EVAN I DAVIS   seal

Recognr: in Cur Comr Rappa 5 die Janry 1664
            Test ROBT. DAVIES Cl Cur

p.   Reced this 5th December 1664 of Mr. WILLIAM HODGKINS in part the sum of
93   Twenty two thousand pounds of tobacco I say reced p order for the account of
            SAML. SLANY
Test RALEIGH TRAVERS,   p GILES CALE
        EDWARD DALE
Recognr in Cur Com Rappa 5 die Janry 1664

pp.   KNOW ALL MEN by these presents that I HENRY REEVES of WARWICK QUICK in
93-   the ILE OF WHITE COUNTY in Virga: do hereby these presents assigne ordaine
94   & make & in my steed & place put & constitute my Loving Friend ROBT: TOMLIN
            of Rappa: County in Virga: Planter my true & lawfull attorny for me & in my
stead & place & to my use to ask sue for levy require recover & receive of all & every
person whatsoever all & every such debts & demands consisting either in goods monys
wrighteings chattels or any other thing or things whatsoever that are now due unto
me or at any day or daystime or times hereafter be due unto me or any other way belonging to me by an manner of ways or means whatsoever giveing & granting unto my
said Attorny by the Tenor of these presents my full and whole power in and about the
premises and upon the receipt of any such sums wrighteings or any other deeds whatsoever acquittances or any other discharges for me or in my name to make seal and deliver and all and every other act and acts in the Law whatsoever needful and necessary
to be done in or abt. the premises for the recovery of any such Debts dues or demands
whatsoever aforesaid for me and in my name to do execute and perform as fully largely
and amply in every respect to all intents as I my self might or could do if I were personally present and further as my sd Attorny shall see cause by virtue of these presents to authorize one or more under him to act in all things as fully as he himself is
hereby impowered to do ratifying and confirming all and whatsoever my said Attorny
shall lawfully do or cause to be done in and about the Exo. of the same by Virtue of these
presents. In Witness whereof I have set my hand and seale this 24th day of Jany 1664
in presence of ROBT. GOODYEAR,   HENRY REEVES   seal
        JOHN HARRIS
Recordr: x die Janry 1664

pp.   KNOW ALL MEN by these presents that I JOHN POOLE do constitute & ordaine my
94-   trusty & welbeloved Friend QUINTAN SHEREMAN to be my true and lawfull At-
95   torny to answer anything that shall be alledged agt me by JOHN or GEORGE KIL-
            MAN or either of them or their attornys and to acknowledge Judgement in my
behalf and further Witness my hand this 7th day of January 1664
Testis the hand of MARY ⨏ POOLE,   JOHN POOLE
        RICHD. GLOVER

pp.   BY THIS PUBLICK INSTRUMT. or Proclamation or Letter of Procuration or Letter
95-   of Attorney be it known and manifest unto all people that on the One and Twen-
96   tieth day of the Month of October Ao. Dom. 1662 Stilo Anglia before me
            FREDERICKE IXEM sole Notary and Tabellion Publick to and for our Sovereign
Lord the King and admitted and sworn dwelling in the City of LONDON and in ye presence of the Witnesses after named personally appeared SAML. SLAINI of LONDON,
Grocer, unto me Notary well known and hath made and ordained & in his steed and

place put and constituted and by these presents doth make GILES CALE of LONDON, Grocer. and SAML. GRIFFIN of Rappa: in Virga. Planter Joyntly and severally his true and lawfull Attorneys and assignes giving unto them joyntly and severally full power and authority and special charge for in the name and to the use of him Constituant to ask demand levy recover and receive of WILLIAM HODGKINS of Rappa: in Virga: Planter or of his heirs goods wheresoever they shall be found or of any other person whatsoever all and singular such sums of money debts goods wares merchandizes effects and things whatsoever as the sd WILLIAM HODGKINS or the said other persons or any of them do owe and are indebted unto him Constituant be it by Bill booke obligation specialty account covenants promises or otherwise by any ways or means whatsoever nothing excepted or reserved with all costs damges and Interests of the receipts acquittance or other sufft. discharges in the name of him Constituant to make seale and deliver and if need be for the premises to appear and the person of the sd Constituant to represent in all Courts and before all Lords Justices and to pursue implead seize attack arrest imprison and to condemn and out of prizon againe when need shall be to deliver likewise one Attorney or more with like or lymitted power under them or either of them to make and substitute and at their or either of their pleasures to revoke & genly. in and concerning the premises and the dependances thereof to conclude and execute and determine all and whasoever the sd Constituant himself might or could do if he were personally present the sd Constituant promising to have and hold for good time and of value all and whatsoever his said Attorney or either of them their or either of their substitutes shall lawfully do or procure to be done in or abt. the premises by virtue of these presents. In Witness whereof the sd Constituant hath hereunto put his hand and seale in the presents of WILLM. SCORY and JOHN STONEHILL my Clerkes Witnesses

SAML: SLANY   seal

in presents of us RICH. LEE
         THO: JAMES. JOHN LEE
Recordatr. attestation rogatus FRED. IXEM Not Publ.
Recordatr in Com Rappa 30 die Jany 1665
                         p ROBT. DAVIS Cl Cur

p.   THESE PRESENTS Witnesseth that I ROGER OVERTON doth constitute and appoint
97   my Friend HENRY CREIGHTON to be my Attorney in a Suit depending between the
        said OVERTON and Mr. THOMAS BOWLER and what my sd Attorney shall doe in the
premises I the sd ROGER OVERTON will ratify and confirm as Witness my hand the 3 day
of January 1664
Testis HENRY ꝉ WOODNOTE.   ROGER ꝛꝺ OVERTON
       THOMAS | LANNE
Recordatr: 30 die Janry 1665

p.   I VALENTINE ALLEN doe acknowledge by these presents that I have for and in
97   the behalf of myself and my heirs bargained sold and firmly set to sale unto
        WILLIAM HODGSON and his heirs for ever Fifty acres of land next adjoining to
the land that WILLIAM HODGSON formerly bought of the sd VALENTINE ALLEN and for
and in consideration of five hundred pounds of tobacco and caske to me in hand paid at
the signeing and sealing hereof do promise to acknowledge the same in Court whensoever thereunto lawfully called. Witness my hand and seale this 20th 9ber 1663, and
Moreover to procure the consent of my Wife to these premises
Test ALEX: FLEMING.   VALENTINE ALLEN   seal
        PETER REIMAS

I MARY ALLEN do give my consent to what my Husband hath above assigned to. Witness my hand and seal Xber 30th 1664

Test HENRY ELLIOT,
     JOHN ∓ SPEED   MARY ∧∧ ALLEN

p.   KNOW ALL MEN by these presents that I VALENTINE ALLEN doe constitute and
98   appoint my Loving Friend HENRY ELIOT to acknowledge for me and in my name
     a Conveyance of Land sould unto WILLIAM HODGSON and what my sd Attorny
doth herein I give him as much and full power as if I were personally present. Witness my hand this 30th Xber 1664

Test JOHN ∓ SPEED,
     JOHN CARPENTER   VALENTINE ALLEN
Recognr in Cur Com Rappa 5 die Martii 1664

pp.   TO ALL TO WHOM these presents shall come I WM. LANE of the County of Rappa.
98- Merchant for and in consideration of the sum of Nine thousand pounds of good
100 tobacco and caske to me in hand paid by THOMAS BOWLER, Mercht., at and before
     the sealing and delivery hereof do by these presents bargain sell assigne and
set over unto the said THOMAS BOWLER and COMPANY their Exors. Admrs. and assignes
all that Plantation and Land thereunto belonging together with all houses, Edifices
buildings Orchards Gardens and all appurtenances whatsoever thereunto belonging or
any wise appertaining or which hath been heretofore accepted reputed or taken to be
any part thereof sd premises were heretofore in the Tenour possession or occupation of
JOHN PAINE and lately purchased of the sd JOHN PAINE by me the sd WILLIAM LANE to
have and to hold the sd Plantation and Land and all other the premises with the appurtenances unto the sd THOMAS BOWLER and Company their Exors. and assignes for and
during the term of ten thousand years fully to be compleat and ended yealding and
paying therefore yearly unto the sd WILLIAM LANE his heirs and assignes One pepper
Corne at the Feast of St. Michael the Archangell if it shall be Lawfully demanded and I
the sd WILLIAM LANE for me my heirs doth promise and agree with ye sd THOMAS BOWLER and Company that they the said THOMAS BOWLER and Company their Exrs. and assignes shall and lawfully may at all times hereafter quietly and peaceably hold and enjoy the Plantation and Land and all other the premises without the let interruption vexation trouble or denyall of me the sd WILLIAM LANE my heirs or assignes or of any
other person whatsoever Provided always and upon this Condition Nevertheless that if
the said WILLIAM LANE my heirs and Admrs. shall well and truly pay or cause to be
paid unto the sd THOMAS BOWLER and Company their Exrs. or assignes the full just
quantity of Nine thousand pounds of good sound Merchantable tobacco and Caske clear
of ground leaves and trash upon the 10th day of December next ensuing the date hereof
at and upon the Plantation whereon I the said WILLIAM LANE now liveth that then this
present wrighting and everything therein contained shall be utterly void and of no
effect to all intents and purposes anything herein contained to the Contrary Notwithstanding. In Witness I the sd WILLIAM LANE have hereunto set my hand and seal this
19th day of January Ao. 1662

in presence of us JOHN WEIR,
     W. GRANGER   WILLIAM LANE   seal

  And the said WILLIAM LANE do ingage myself my heirs or assignes to acknowledge
these presents in open Court held for the County of Rappa.

     W. GRANGER,   WILLIAM LANE
Recognr: in Cur Com Rappa 6 die May 1663
Recordatr 10 die   Test W. GRANGER

Received this 5th of January 1663 of Mr. WILLIAM LANE the just quantity of Five thousand Two hundred and fifty it being in part of this within specified bond tobo and caske I say reced p me

                                        THOMAS BOWLER   5250

Received this 15th of November 1664 more in part of this bond the Sum of Two thousand two hundred and fifty nine I say reced by me

                                        THOMAS BOWLER   2259

I Underwritten and Company do for us our heirs Exrs. and Admrs. and Assignes transfer and turn over all our right title and Interest of this within mentioned deed unto WILLM. LANE his heirs Exrs. Admrs. or assignes. In Witness whereof I the sd THOMAS BOWLER and Company accordingly set my hand and seal this 18th of January 1664 in presence of us THOMAS HAWKINS

              ROBT. DAVIS   THOS: BOWLER   seal

Recognr: in Cur Com Rappa 18 die January 1664

                        Test ROBT. DAVIS Cl Cur

p.   The Mark of the Hoggs & Catle of JOHN JAMES (Vizt) A crop in the right ear & a
101   slit in the left ear & an overkeel with the under part of the said Left ear a litle
        cut of
Recorded 10 Aprill 1665   Test RD Cl Cur

        ELIZA: WILSONs marke is cropt in both ears & a slit in the left ear & two notches under the right ear
Recorded 10th April 1665   Test RD Cl Cur

        The mark of the hoggs & catle of NICHO: COPELAND is Vizt: the right ear cropt & a slit in the Crop the left ear a peice taken out above & below almost like an overkeel
Recorded 10th April 1665   Test RD Cl Cur

        The mark of the Catle & hoggs of DENNIS SWILLIVANT Vizt. a Swallow fork in the right ear & a half moone in ye left ear
Recorded 13th April 1665

        The Mark of the Hoggs & Catle of Mr. FRANCIS DOUGHTY is a crop in the right Ear & a slit in the left Eare

        The Mark of the Hoggs & Catle of ENOCH DOUGHTY Vizt. Cropt on the right ear & a slit in the Crop & a slit in the left ear
Recorded 10th Aprill 1665   Test ROBT: DAVIES Cl Cur preda:

        The Mark of the Hoggs & catle of NICHOS: CATLET Vizt. two crops & a slit in each ear & an underkeel in ye right ear
Recorded 3d February 1665

        The Mark of the Hoggs & Catle of JOHN LAMPART is Vizt. a swallow forke in the right ear & a popler Leaf in the left ear
Recordatr. 3 February 1665

p.   The Mark of the Hoggs & Catle of JOHN MATLYN is Vist. Cropt in the right ear &
102   two slits in the Crop & the left ear Slit right down with a peice taken out of the

same eare near the form of a half moon

Recorded 24th Febry 1665

The Marke of the Catle & Hoggs of WILLIAM BRUCE is Vizt. A Crop in each ear &
two slits in each crop

Recordatr March the 14 1665.

Test ROBT: DAVIES Cl Cur

pp.   TO ALL XPIAN PEOPLE to whom this present Instrumt. of wrighting shall come
102-   know ye that I JOHN AYRES of the County of Rappa. & Parish of Sittenbourne in
103   Virga: for divers good causes & valuable considerations me thereunto moveing
        & more especially for & in consideration of the sume of nine thousand pounds of
good tobacco & caske to me in hand paid with one case of Drams at & before the ensealing & delivery of these presents the receipt whereof I do hereby acknowledge with
my full content by ROBT. DAVIES of the same County & Parish aforesaid have given sold
& confirmed & do by these presents for me my heirs give sell & confirme unto ye sd
ROBT. DAVIES Five hundred Sixty & One acres of land situate lying and being on the
South side of RAPPA: RIVER & County & Parish aforesd part thereof being the one half
or moiety cont. 366 acres of land in my possession & Whereon I lately lived & devided in
presence of ye Neighbourhood the residue being 378 acres which I lately took up & adjoyning on the afd. land & the lands of the sd ROBT: DAVIES & JOHN MEADE to have and
to hold the sd Five hundred Sixty one acres of land with all & singular the houses out
houses Orchards gardens & plantation with the appurtenances thereon from me the sd
JOHN AYRES my heirs Exrs. & assignes to him ye sd ROBT. DAVIS his heirs Exrs. or assignes for ever to the Sole & proper use & behoof of him the sd ROBT. DAVIES his heirs
or assignes furthermore & I the sd JOHN AYRES for my self my heirs do hereby promise & agree with the sd ROBT: DAVIES his heirs & assignes that he shall & may from
time to time have hold possess & enjoy the sd 561 acres of land with all & every the premises with the appurtenaces & every part & parcell thereof by these presents granted
without the hindrance denyall ejection of me the said JOHN AYRES my heirs Exrs. or
assignes or any other persons wtsoever lawfully Claimeing the same or any parte or
parcell thereof the sd ROBT: DAVIS his heirs Exrs Admrs or assignes yeilding and
paying & dischargeing the rites & services hereof due & of right accustomed. In Witness whereof the sd JOHN AYRES have hereunto set his hand & seal this 11th day of July
1666.

in presents of us ALEX. FLEMING,   JOHN AIRES   seal
        JOHN WEIR

  This Deed of Sale was the day & year abovesd acknowledged before us by JOHN AYRES to
ROBT: DAVIES & his heirs Exrs. Admrs. & assignes for ever withall true intents &
meaing acording to Law & desired to be recorded in the records of the County of Rappa

                                ALEX. FLEMING
                                JOHN WEIR

Recordatr. in Com Rappa xii die July 1666

                Test ROBT: DAVIS Cl Cur

pp.   KNOW ALL MEN by these presents that I PETER BAWCOMB of the County of Rappa
104-   do hereby acknowledge and confess that I have bargained and sould unto
105   RICHARD BREDGAR of the County afsd his heirs and assignes Six hundred acres
        of land more or less for a valuable consideration to my own content already in
hand reced the sd land being two third parts of a tract of land of Nine hundred acres
Pattented in the name of RICHARD LAWRENCE and THOMAS WILLIAMSON and EVAN

DAVIS and by the sd THOMAS WILLIAMSON and EVAN DAVIS sold conveyed and acknowledged unto me the said BAWCOMB as by the Records of Rappa. Court may appear the sd
land lying and being on the South side of RAPPA RIVER and in Rappa. County beginning at a marked white Oak standing on the Eastward side of a WHITE MARSH at the head
of a branch issuing out of the DRAGGON SWAMP and crossing MATTAPONY UPPER PATH
thence running Southerly along the sd Branch to ye DRAGGON SWAMP thence Easterly
alongst the said Swamp to another branch thereof along the sd branch to a marked tree
standing in MATTAPONY PATH thence alongst the PATH NW to the first specified place
the which land with all rights and priviledges thereunto belonging I the said PETER
BAWCOMB do acknowledge and in the possession deliver unto him the said RICHARD
BRIDGAR his heirs and admrs and assignes for ever to be by him and them quietly enjoyed and possessed for ever and further I do hereby forever quit all claime title or interest to the sd Land or any part thereof from me the sd PETER BAWCOMB my heirs or
assignes for ever and do hereby bind my self my heirs or assignes for ever to make
good the sale of the sd land and to keep him the said RICHARD BRIDGAR his heirs and
assignes harmless and Indemnified from all manner of trouble or molestation whatsoever from all or any persons whatsoever that shall hereafter lay claime unto the sd
land or any part thereof in the penalty of the paymt. of ten thousand pounds of tobacco
and cask unto him the sd RICHD. BRIDGAR his heirs or assignes to this my act and deed
I have set my hand & seal this 12th day of February 1665
in presents of THO: PATTISON,   PETER BAWCOMB   seal
          JACOB JENNIFER
Recognr: in Cur Comr Rappa 7 die Martii Ao. 1665

p.   KNOW ALL MEN by these presents that I PETER BAWCOMB of Rappa. do hereby
105   constitute & appoint my Friend THOMAS PATTISON for me & in my name to ack-
        nowledge a conveyance for Six hundred acres of land in and at any Court held
in Rappa County within six months according to Law the sd Conveyance bearing date
herewith giveing my sd Attorny as full & ample power in & concerning the premises as
if myself were personally present or as is in any Letter of Attorney expressed as witness my hand & Seal this 12th day of February 1665
in presents of JACOB JENIFER,   PETER BAWCOMBE   seal
          MARY X DAVIS

pp.   TO ALL CHRISTIAN PEOPLE to whom this present writing shall come SAML:
105-   PARRY of the Parish of Farnham in ye County of Rappa. sendeth Greeting in our
106   Lord God everlasting Know ye that I SAML. PARRY for good consideration me
        thereunto moveing & for & in consideration of the Speciall love & singular
affection which I always bear unto my Loving Friend FRANCIS BROWN of PISCATACON
CREEK in the Parish afd. Planter have given granted & aliened delivered & confirmed
unto the said FRANCIS BROWNE his heirs & admrs. for Ever free egress & regress to that
ILAND GROUND or parcell of land commonly knowne or called by ye name of the
WADING POINT situate & being near the Plantation now in the Tenour of NATHL. BAXTER
on PISCATACON CREEK above mentioned to have & to hold to clear build & make any use
of whatsoever for his own necessary occasion wth priviledges I give unto him the said
FRANCIS BROWN from me my heirs Exrs: Admrs: without any molestation or trouble to
FRANCIS BROWN his heirs for ever warranting & confirming my sd Gift as also this In-
strument of assurance or Deed of Gift & all things else thereunto belonging from me
SAML. PARRY my heirs Exrs. Admrs: & other assignes whatsoever. In Witness whereof
I have hereunto set my hand & Seal this 25th day of 7ber Ao: Dom: 1665

in presence of THO. + HARPER.   SAML: PARRY   seal
     RI: GLOVER
Recognr: in Cur Com Rappa 7 die Martii Ao: 1665

p.   The Mark of the Hoggs & Catle of Capt. THOS. HAWKINS Vizt. Cropt in the left ear
106   & a swallow fork in the right ear
    Recordr: 10 die Martii Ao. 1665   Test RD Cl Cur

    The Mark of Hoggs & Catle of Capt. HUMPHRY BOOTH Vizt. a half moone under
each ear & a Slit down each ear
Recordr: 10 die Martii Ao: 1665

    The Mark of the hoggs & Catle of RO: PAYNE Cl is the flower de luce on the left
ear & the Staple on the right ear
Recordatr: x die Novembris 1667
               Test RO: PAYNE Cl Cur

pp.   WHEREAS I HENRICK LUCAS have twenty & five acres of land whereon THO:
106- THORP is now seated these presents shall oblige me the sd LUCAS if the sd THORP
107   buy not the same of me then Capt. ALEX. FLEMING shall have the refusing
    thereof & to pay Eight hundred pounds of tobo: & caske for ye same & no more
Witness my hand this 13th day of September 1666
    Test Sept. 1666

p.   IN THE NAME OF GOD Amen. I THOMAS WRIGHT being at present weak in body
107   but perfect in memory do make this my last Will & Testamt. I Do bequeath my
    Soul to Almighty God my Creator & my body to the Earth to be buryed after a
decent manner & my worldly goods I bestow as followeth I do make my Loving Wife
JANE WRIGHT my Sole Exr: of all my whole Estate after my debts be paid only I desire
that my female Catle be equally divided the one half to run for the use of my Daughter
ELIZA: WRIGHT & the other half to my Loving Wife Likewise I do appoint Mr. JOHN
WASHINGTON Overseer of this my last Will & Testamt. dated this 23th: Octobr: 1664
Test ROGER + RICHARDSON.   THO: TR WRIGHT
    ROBT. SISSON
Recordatr: 10 die May 1666   Test RD Cl Cur

pp.   KNOW ALL MEN by these presents that I ROBERT SISSON of the County of Rappa
107- Planter & AMY my Wife for & in consideration of the sum of Seven thousand
109   pounds of tobacco & caske to me in hand paid by QUINTAN SHERMAN of the
    County aforesd at & before the sealing & delivery of these presents the receipt
whereof I do acknowledge have granted bargained sold & confirmed & by these presents do grant sell & confirm unto the said QUINTAN SHERMAN his heirs & assigns the
moyety or halfendale of all that Plantacon & tract of land wch I the said ROBT. SISSON
bought of Mr. HUMPHRY BOOTH together with the moyety of all houses edifices buildings gardens orchards lands & the moyety of all other the Premises with the apptence
belonging to the same being in the County of Rappa. & on the North side of the said
River of RAPPA & now in the tenure possession or occupacon of me the said ROBT. SIS-
SON To have & to hold the said premises by these presents granted with the appurtenances & every part thereof unto said QUINTAN SHERMAN his heirs & assignes for ever
to the use & behoof of the sd QUINTAN SHERMAN his heirs & assignes for evermore to be
holden of the Chief Lord of the Fee or Fees thereof by the Rents & Services therefore

first due & of right accustomed and I the said ROBERT SISSON do for me my heirs promise with the said QUINTAN SHERMAN his heirs & assignes shall at all times hereafter
quietly & peaceably hold occupy & enjoy the said Premises by these presents granted
with the appurtenances without the Incumbrance or denyal of me the said ROBERT SIS-
SON my heirs or assignes or of any other person or persons whatsoever & I the said
ROBERT SISSON do for me my heirs & admrs. promise grant & agree with the said QUIN-
TAN SHERMAN his heirs & assignes by these presents that I ye said ROBERT SISSON my
heirs shall & will at all times hereafter warrant & defend the said Premises by these
presents granted with the appurtenances unto the said QUINTAN SHERMAN his heirs &
assigns for ever agt all persons whatsoever. In Witness whereof I have hereunto set
my hand & seal this 2 January 1663

                                                ROBERT SISSON   seal
                                                AMY ✗ SISSON   seal

Acknowledged in Court die Second 1663

p.   THESE PRESENTS Witnesseth that I QUINTAN SHERMAN of the County of Rappa.
109   in Virga. Planter for & in consideration of the sum of Five thousand five hun-
        dred pounds of tobacco & Caske to me in hand paid or by bills secured of ANDREW
HERBERT of the same County have & do assign transfer & make over all my right title &
Interest of ye within specyfied conveyance unto the said ANDREW HERBERT To have &
to hold the Premises & every part thereof to him & his heirs from me & my heirs for
evr. In Witness whereof I have hereunto set my hand & seal this 5th day of 8br 1665
in presence of us THOS. FRESHWATER,   QUINTAN+ SHERMAN seal
        ROBT. DAVIS
Recognitr in Cur Com Rappa 3 die 9bris 1665

p.   The Names of the Gentn. of the VESTRY of the PARISH of FARNHAM in Rappa.
109   County as they were sworn the third day of November 1665
        Vizt Mr. FRANCIS DOUGHTY, Minister
        Lt. Coll. THOMAS GOODRICH   JAMES SAMPFORD
        ANTHO. NORTH   JOHN GRIGORY
        THOMAS BUTTON   ROBERT BAYLEY
        THOS. ROBINSON   JOHN WILLIAMS
Recordd. this x die 9bris 1665.
                p. ROBT. DAVIS Cl Cur

p.   The Mke of JOHN MEADERS Son of THOMAS MEADERS upon HODGKINS CREEK one
110   black heiffer one calf black coloured One Sow Pigg this mark is the flower de
        luce on the left ear & on the right ear a half moon & a slitt this to be recorded
for JOHN MEADERS with both male & female increase

        The Mke of the hoggs & Catle of GREGORY GLASCOCKE Vizt. the right ear begin-
ning at the root & cutt tapering the top of the underside of the right ear cut tapering
from the root to the top cutting the top of the upper side of the left ear cut in the same
form
Recorded 22 Febry 1665   pr RD Cl Cur

p.   The mrk of THO. GLASCOCKE is the same Mrk as his Brot. GRIGY. only with two
110   nicks under the left ear
        Recorded 22 Febry 1665   pr RD Cl Cur

The mrk of JOHN GLASCOCKE is the same Mrk as his Bro. GRIGS. only with two
nicks under the left ear.
     Recordat 22 Feb 1665

     THOS. FRESHWATERs mrk is a swallow fork & an underkeel in the left ear & a
crop in the right ear
Recorded 22 Feb 1665   p RD Cl Cur

p.   I do authorize & appoint Mr. JNO. APLETON to receive the above menconed Debts
110   they being justly due to me & what he shall lawfully do herein shall be as firm
       as if I were present as witness my hand this nineteenth of April 1664
Test ELIAS FLOWER   WILLM. W WATSON
    JOHN HOBBS
Record p Mr. JNO. APLETON 3 Janry 1665
           Test RD C Cur Rappa.

pp.   KNOW ALL MEN by these presents that I ANDREW GILSON of the County of Rappa.
111-   in Virga. Gent for & in consideration of the sum of Twenty & five thousand
112   pounds of good sufficient tobacco without trash at & before the sealing & deli-
      very of these presents satisfied & paid & by me my heires Exrs. Admrs. & assigns
acknowledged to be satisfied & paid have fully clearly & absolutely given sold & confirmed & by these presents do give grant sell & confirm unto JOHN WEIR his heirs Exrs.
Admrs. & assigns for ever a certain MILL contained within a MILL HOUSE scituate
lyeing & being at the head of a Creek goeing out of the River of RAPPA. by computa-
tion WSW about five miles commonly called Mr. GILSONS CREEK with all & singular the
appurtenances thereunto belonging used occupied & appertaining in any wise thereunto To have and to hold the said MILL HOUSE with the MILL therein contained & all &
singular the water Course and water Courses thereunto belonging & all & singular the
benefitts proffits and comodities whatsoever to him the said JOHN WEIR his heirs & assigns for ever to the only ppr use & behoof of him forevermore and the said ANDREW
GILSON for himself his heirs doth covenant and grant with the said JOHN WEIR his
heirs & assigns that he the said ANDREW GILSON hath good title full power & rightfull
authority to grant sell & confirm the said premises unto ye said JOHN WEIR his heirs for
ever according to the true meaning of these presents and the said ANDREW GILSON for
himself his heirs doth promise & grant to & with the said JOHN WEIR that he his heirs &
assigns and every of them at the special Instance & at the proper costs & charges of the
said JOHN WEIR his heirs will uphold fulfill maintain & compleat this present Instrument of Enfeoffment agst all & every person whatsoever wch may or would hereafter
claim any title to the premises from or under the said ANDREW GILSON his heirs or any
person whatsoever wch may or would hereafter lay claim to the same. In Witness
whereof the party above menconed have to these presents set his hand & seal this
Eighth day of Febry Anno Dom 1665
in presence of us HUM. BOOTH,   ANDREW GILSON   seal
    W. ABERNETHY
Recognitr in Cur Com Rappa 8 die Feb 1665

pp.   TO ALL TO WHOM &c. Now know ye that I the sd Sr. WM. BERKELEY Knt. Governor
112-   &c do with the consent of the Council of State accordingly give & grant unto Mr.
113   THOMAS CHETWOOD Two thousand acres of land on the Southside of RAPPA RIVER
      in the Freshes of the said River beginning at the head of a small Creek called by
the name of MOONS CREEK & runing South 240 poles beginning on the North side of a

main branch & S. 200 p. on the S. side of the Main Swamp & into the woods parralel as the said Swamp runns Westerly thence Northerly Ely to the place where it first began to have and to hold &c to be held &c yeilding & paying &c Provided &c Given at JAMES CITY under my hand & the Seal of the Colony this first of August 1665 Annoq Dom Regis Caroli 2d 17th

Recordatr. 10th Augt. 1665   WILLIAM BERKELEY
     Test PHILL LUDWELL Cl Off:

p.   KNOW ALL MEN by these presents that I THOMAS CHETWOOD do for me my heirs
113   Exrs. Admrs. & assigns alien enfeoff & sett over unto THOMAS FRESHWATER his
     heirs Exrs. admrs. or assigns six hundred acres of this within menconed land with all rights proffits priviledges according to the Pattent with warranty of all & every the premises from all manner of persons that shall lay any claim or Interest to the premises or to any part thereof. In Witness whereof I the said CHETWOOD have hereunto set my hand this 8th of Febry 1665

Testes GEORGE MORRISS,   THOS. CHETWOOD
     THOS. WRIGHT
Recognitr in Cur Com Rappa 8 die Feb 1665
          Test ROBT. DAVIS Cl Cur

All the Records in this Book were faithfully Examined with the OLD RECORD BOOK by Order of Essex County Court.

               By me
                     W. BEVERLEY Cl Cur

---

pp.   IN THE NAME OF GOD Amen &c. I LUKE BILLINGTON of Farnham Parish in Rappa
114- County being of sound and perfect memory thanks be given to God therefore doe
116   make this my last Will and Testament in manner and forme as followeth Vizt.
     Imp. I give and bequeath unto my beloved Wife BARBARY BILLINGTON the house wherein I now dwell with all moveables and unmoveables and lands belonging thereunto belonging to the sd Plantation with all the Cattle belonging to me as Mares and Horses Sheepes and all the graine as Corne and Wheat with Servants and all my household goodes within doors and without during the term of hir naturall life and after hir decease the land to fall to my Son LUKE BILLINGTON and his heirs for ever and I doe oblige my sd Wife to provide and give unto my sd Daughter ELIZABETH at hir day of Marriage either a Man Servant or a Maid Servant for the terme of time as Servants come into this Country to Serve
     Item I give unto my Sonne LUKE BILLINGTON the MOUNTAIN FIELDS wherein now RICHARD PEACOCK liveth to him and his heirs for ever and in case he dieth without issue then the sd Land to be devided between his Fower Sisters heere nominated being ELITIA and ELIZABETH and JANE and BARBARY my Daughters and in case that any or either of my sd Daughters shall die without issue that the sd Land belong to the Survivour or Survivours
     Item I doe obleige my Sonne LUKE to give and deliver at the day of Marriage of my Daughter JANE and BARBARY to each of them a Man Servant or a Maid Servant for the full time and terme of years as Servants serve their lawfull apprenticeship in this Country
     Item I give and bequeath unto my Daughter ELITIA three hundred and fifty acres of land belonging to the MOUNTAINE FIELDS as by a Pattent purchased appeareth and if my said Daughter dieth without issue that then the sd Land fall and be devided

between my three Daughters ELIZABETH, JANE and BARBARY and in case any of them die without issue to fall to the Survivor or Survivors

Item I give unto my Daughter MARY a peece of plate to the value of thirty shillings and to her Sonne, my Grand Child, WILLIAM DANIEL, a yew with a yew lamb by her side

Item I do further appoint and obleige my Wife to pay and satisfie all or any just debts wch shall be made appear that I owe either by obligation or account

Item I make my Wife BARBARY BILLINGTON my whole and Sole Executrix of this my last Will and Testamt. and further I desire my trusty and well beloved Friends Mr. WILLIAM TRAVERS and Mr. GYLES CALE to be Trustees of this my Will and Testament that to their power as much as in them lyeth it be performed. In Witness whereof to these prsents I have set my hand and Seale this 13th day of November 1671

Further Dr. JOHN RUSSELL to be a Trustee to this my Last Will with Mr. WILLIAM TRAVERS and Mr. GILES CALE

Sealed & delivered in the presence of us　　　　　　LUKE BILLINGTON　　seal
HENRY SHEARES,
JOHN RUSSELL
Recordatr in Com Rappa　May the xx3th 1672

　　　　　　　　Test EDMUND CRASK Cl Cur Com Rappa

pp.　HENRY SHEARS aged 35 years or thereabouts, JOHN RUSSELL aged 26 years or
116-　thereabts. Sworn and Examined say that they saw the above named LUKE BIL-
117　LINGTON signe Seale and Publish this writing whereunto his hand & seale is
　　　annexed as his Last Will and Testamt. and that then he was in perfect mind and
Memory to the best of their knowledge and further say not

　　　　　　　　　　　　　　　HENRY SHEARES
　　　　　　　　　　　　　　　JOHN RUSSELL

p.　IN THE NAME OF GOD Amen I SOLOMON MARTIN being Sick and Weake in body but
117　of perfect Sence and memorie blessed be God for it do make my Last Will & Testa-
　　　ment in manner and form following

First I bequeath my Soul to God who gave it

Next I bequeath my Body to the Earth to be decently buried at the discretions of my Friends Trusting in the merritts of the Lord & Saviour Jesus Christ for a joyfull resurrection of the same unto Life eternall And for my worldly goods I dispose of them as followeth

I doe wholly give & bequeath all my Estate both reall and personall unto my well beloved Friend GEORGE MOTT and to his three Children ELIZABETH, MARGARET and ANNE all the living Creatures as well Cattle as Horses and Mares to be devided between them at the discretion of their Father and doe hereby make my aforesd Friend GEORGE MOTT my Sole Executor of this my Last Will and Testament revoaking and makeing void hereby all former Wills. In Witness whereof I have hereunto set my hand & Seale this 28th of October 1671

p.　IN THE NAME OF GOD Amen Augt. the 27th: 1670. First I give my Soul into the
118　hands of Christ my Redeemer next my body to a Christian Buriall. And for what
　　　worldly Estate the Lord hath bin pleased to make me Steward of I give and be-
queath unto my well beloved Friend EDWARD LEWIS making him my whole Executor and in Witness whereof I have sett my hand & Seale being in health and perfect

memory

Witnesse WILLIAM N DAVIS,   DAVID THOMAS   seal
    DAVID HUDNALL

These may satisfie whom it may concern that DAVID HUDNALL hath made oath before me that he did see DAVID THOMAS signe and Seale this Will and owne it to be his act & deed

Sworn before me the 3d of Januarie 1671   DAVID HUDNALL
    JOHN ROGERS

Recordatr 3d die Junii 1672

            Test EDMUND CRASK Cl Cur Com Rappa

pp.   IN THE NAME OF GOD Amen the 8th day of May 1672 I WALTER WILLIAMS being
119-   sick in Body but in good and perfect memory thanks bee to Almighty God and
120   calling to remembrance the uncertainty of this life and that all flesh must yield
        to death when it shall please God to call doe make constitute ordaine and declare
this my Last Will and Testament in manner and forme following revoaking and annulling all other Wills either by word of Mouth or writing

And First I comit my Soule into my Saviour and Redeemer in whom and by the merritts of Christ I trust and believe assuredly to be saved and that my Soul with my body at the resurrection shall rise again with joy and my body to be buried in decent manner

And for the settling of my temporall estate I doe order give and dispose the same in manner and forme following

Imprimis I give unto ELIZABETH THATCHER a Cow also I give and bequeath unto JOHN CAMMOCK a young Heifer to them and their heirs for ever

Item I give and bequeath the land I bought of JOHN MEADER and HENRY PETERS wch SAML JOHNSON hath a half in it to WARWICK CAMMOCK and his heirs for ever paying the remainder of the Tobacco that is due for it and I make and constitute the sd CAM-MOCK Executor of this my Will and desire that all my just debts be paid.

In Witnesse whereof I have hereunto sett my hand and Seale this day & year above written. Also I give to SILVESTER THATCHER a Steire and to MATHEW THATCHER a young Heifer.

Sealed & delivered in the presence of us   WALTER X WILLIAMS seale
    PETER DUNNIVAN
      SAMUELL JOHNSON

Wee PETER DUNNIVAN and SAMUELL JOHNSON doe heere dispose that this within written Will is the Last Will and Testament of WALTER WILLIAMS and noe other Will to our Knowledge and that he was in perfect memory when the same was made
    PETER DUNNIVAN
      SAMUELL JOHNSON

Jurantr in Cu 3 die Julii 1672

Recordatr xxii die ejusd

            Test EDMUND CRASK Cl Cur Com Rappa

pp.   IN THE NAME OF GOD Amen the Twenty eighth day of May in the Twenty fourth
120-   year of the Reign of our most gratious Soveraigne Lord CHARLES the Second by
124   the Grace of God King of England Scotland France & Ireland defender of the
        faith &c Anno Dom 1672 I THOMAS WRIGHT of MORATICON CREEKE in the County
of Rappa Planter being Sick and Weake in body but of sound and perfect memory praise be given to God for the same and knowing the uncertainty of the life on Earth and

being desirous to settle things in order doe make this my Last Will and Testament in manner and forme following That is to say first and principally I commend my Soul to Almighty God my Creator assuredly beleiving that I shall receive full pardon and free remission of all my Sinns and to be saved by the Pretious death and merritts of my blessed Saviour & Redeemer Christ Jesus and my body to the Earth from whence it was taken to bee buried in such decent and Christian buriall as my Executor hereafter named shall think meete and convenient and as touching such worldly Estate as the Lord in Mercy hath lent me my Will and meaning is the same shall be imployed and bestowed as heereafter by this my Will is expressed and first I doe declare and appoint this my last Will & Testament recalling renouncing frustrating and making void all Wills by me formerly made

Item I give and bequeath unto my Wife MARY WRIGHT all and every the goods chattles Cattle whatsoever that she had when I married her to her only use

Item I give and bequeath to WILLIAM BALDWYNs Daughter living with one ISACK STANNOP on the South side of RAPPA RIVER the sume of Six hundred pounds of tobacco to bee laid out upon a Cow for hir use and my will is that my Sonne in Law EDWARD POOLE shall have the laying out of the tobacco and that he sees the Cow recorded with the increase to hir & hir heires for ever

Item I give unto EDWARD RYLYEs Wives Daughter the like sum of Six hundred pounds of tobo: to bee laid out for a Cow for hir my will being that THOMAS MADDISON have the laying out of the tobacco and that he see the Cow recorded with the encrease unto hir and hir heires for ever

Item I give unto my Couzen EDWARD CARTER my young Mare & hir increase and three hundred acres of land joyning upon Mr. HALLs Land and lyeing by Collonel LEEs PATH and sold me by Mr: THOMAS CHETWOOD in part of Satisfaction of One thousand acres which doth appear upon the records of LANCASTER COUNTY

Item I give unto my Sonns in Law THOMAS and ROBERT BRYANT my old Mare to them and their heires for ever and one thousand pounds of tobacco apeece

Item I give unto my Son in Law ROBERT BRIANT one hundred & fifteen acres of land wch lyes by MORATICON MILL being part of two hundred and thirty acres of land Between JOHN CHINE and my Selfe unto him and his heirs forever

Item I give unto my Daughters in Laws Child ELISABETH POOL my old Mares ffoale which fell this prsent yeare and hir increase but if in case the sd ELISABETH POOLL doe decease without issue of her body then the sd Legacy shall return to THOMAS and ROBERT BRIANT and to their heires for ever

Item I give unto BRIAN STOTTs Children my Stone Colt which is at this prsent above one year old and my will is that BRIAN STOTT their Father have the ordering of it as he thinks fitt

Item my will is that all legacies which I have given away bee paid the next Cropp after my decease

And Lastly I doe make my Wife MARY WRIGHT my full and whole Executrix of this my last Will and Testament giving unto her my Servants with all the remainder of my goods chattles cattle and household stuff whatsoever and all my debts which are due unto me she paying my legacys as aforesd and my debts which I owe

In Witness whereof I have hereunto set my hand and Seale to this my last Will and Testament the day and yeare above written
in the prsence of us

    BRIAN STOTT   THOMAS WRIGHT   Seale
      the marke of R B ROBERT BRIAN
Recordatr xxii die Septemb. 1672

                    Test EDMUND CRASK Cl Cur

BRIAN STOTT aged about 45 years and ROBERT BRIANT aged about twenty two years depose and say that they did see THOMAS WRIGHT sign and seale this Will and Testament and that to the best of their knowledge this is the Last Will and Testament of the sd WRIGHT and that he was in perfect sence and memory at the time of the signing heereof

Jurantur in Cu Com Rappa 4 die Septemb

pp.   IN THE NAME OF GOD Amen., The Last Will and Testament of Capt. DAVID MAN-
125-   SELL I being in perfect memory and sence yet Sick and weake in body
127   Item I give my Soul to God that gave it my body to be buried in Christian buriall hoping through the merritts of my deare Saviour to obtain mercy for all my Sins and transgressions

Item I make and ordain and depute my well beloved Friend & nearest Neighbour WILLIAM WHEELER my full and whole Executor puting my whole trust in him my sd Executor to take on himself the same charge and care to bring up and educate my God-child DAVID and to take to himself of the sd DAVID FRISTO his Estate which I now possess or might possess and retaine until the sd FRISTO be come of age if I lived

Item I desire my sd Executor shall truely pay all and every lawfull debt which I stand indebted to any person or persons with my own proper estate

Item I give and bequeath unto my Daughter MARY my Sealed ring

Item I give and bequeath unto my Grandchild MANSELL BLAGRAVE and his heirs and Successors for ever one Tract of land adjoyning to the land of Mr. ROBERT BAYLY on which land standeth a House called the BLOCKHOUSE there being neer two hundred acres

Item I give unto my sd Executor WILLIAM WHEELER the halfe part of my estate that shall appeare to remain after those debts and legacies be deducted out of the whole

Item I give and bequeath unto my sd Grandchild MANSELL BLAGRAVE the other half part of my Estate that shall remaine after the debts and legacies be deducted as abovesd out of the whole

Item I give and bequeath the abovesd remainder of my estate unto the sd WIL-LIAM WHEELER and MANSELL BLAGRAVE or their heires or assignes either to bee devided or sold by my aforesd Executor or by him my sd Executor to bee retained puting in Security for the halfe part to bee delivered when my sd Grandchild cometh to bee of age or whatsoever my sd Executor shall see best for both his and my Grandchilds advantage so putting my whole trust and confidence to him my sd Executor WILLIAM WHEELER to do execute and performe according to the tenor of these prsents it being mine own will and desire

In Witness whereof I have hereunto put my hand this 24th day of July in the year of our Lord God 1672

Witness JONAS PAGE his ⊥P mark   DAVID MANSELL
    MARTHA LEWIS her ✕ mark
Recordatr xxii die Septembr 1672

JONAS PAGE aged Forty seven years and MARTHA LEWIS aged about thirty years depose and say that this is the last Will and Testament of DAVID MANSELL and that they see him sign it and that he was in perfect sence and memory when he signed it

Jurantr in Cu Com Rappa 4 die Septemb 1672

pp.   IN THE NAME OF GOD Amen EDWARD HUTSON his Last Will and Testament lyeing
127- very sick and weake but perfect in Sence & memory commiting of my body to
128   the ground and my Soul to Almighty God Amen

I EDWARD HUTSON do give unto my Son JOHN BARTON two Cows the one called by the name of Young Coale and the other called by the name of Crompell with all the increase for the future more I give unto him three Bills conteining fower thousand pounds of tobacco & cask furthermore I EDWARD HUTSON doe make DOROTHY HUTSON my true and lawfull Wife my whole Executor and all moveables and unmoveables during her life time

Furthermore I do give unto ELIZABETH HOLT one Cow Calfe the first Calfe that falls with all the future increase

So haveing no more to say but committing of my body to the ground and my Soule to the Almighty Amen in the year of our Lord 1672 being the 13th day of March Witnessed by us and

Signed and sealed in presence of us

    ARTHUR HODGES,   EDWARD HUTSON   Seale
    PETER HOPGOOD

ARTHUR HODGES aged thirty three years or thereabouts doth depose and Sweare that this is the last Will and Testament of EDWARD HUTSON and that he was in pfect memory when he signed it

                               ARTHUR HODGES

Juratr in Cur Com Rappa Sexto die Novembris 1672

              Test EDMUND CRASK Cl Cur

pp.   IN THE NAME OF GOD Amen I JOHN DEYOUNG of the County of Rappa and Parish of
129- Farnham being very weake in body but of Sound and perfect memory doe heere
131   make my last Will and Testament as followeth

Imp. I bequeath my Soule to God that gave it in hopes of a sure and certaine resurrection in and through Jesus Christ my Lord and Saviour and my body to be buried in such decent manner as my Friends hereafter named shall think meet and my worldly goods in manner and form following

Item I give unto my Daughter ELIZABETH DEYOUNG two Cowes & all my whole Stock of hoggs which shall happen to be after my decease and also one Steer of fower years old

Item It is my will that the rest of my whole Stock of Cattle both male and feemale bee equally devided between my fower Children Vizt: ELIZABETH, ANN, HONOUR and JOHN DEYOUNG

Item I give unto JOHN DEYOUNG my long Gunn

Item I do moreover give unto my Daughter ELIZABETH my best feather bed with the rugg and blanketts belonging thereunto.

Item I doe give the remainder of my goods & moveables to be equally devided betweene my abovesd Children ELIZABETH, ANNE, JOHN & HONOUR DEYOUNG

Item I give my land unto my Sonne JOHN DEYOUNG

Item It is my will that my Stock nor other Estate bee noe waies removed of the land if possibly it may be prevented

Item It is my will that my Daughter ELIZABETH together with my Bror. in Law GEORGE KNOTT and my Friend THOMAS FRESHWATER doe after my decease take care to see this my last Will and Testamt. in all particulars as neare as may bee performed and first before my legacies bee paid as aforesd my debts bee paid and satisfied and in confirmation of the prmises I have heerunto sett my hand and Seale this 5th of March 1671/2

Signed sealed and published
  in the presence of us ZACHERY ♂ EFFORD   JOHN ℬ DEYOUNG   seale
     WILLIAM DAVIS

Wee the Subscribers doe declare that wee did see JOHN DEYOUNG sign seale and publish
this as his Last Will and Testamt. and that he was then in perfect mind and memory to
the best of our Judgments

                                  WILLIAM DAVIS
                                  ZACHARY ℐ EFFORD

Jurantur in Cu Com Rappa Sexto die Novemb 1672 et Probat

pp.   IN THE NAME OF GOD Amen the Thirtieth day of June 1672 I WILLIAM TUSSLEY
131-   being sick in body but of good and perfect memory thanks bee to Almighty God
132   doe ordaine and declare this my last Will and Testament in manner and form
        following revoaking all other Wills heeretofore by me made
        I give and commit my Soule unto Almighty God my Savioure and redeemer in
whom and by the merit of Jesus Christ I trust and beleive assuredly to bee saved
        And now for the setling of my temporarall Estate as it hath pleased God to bestow
upon me I doe order give and dispose of the same in manner and form following
        I will that all those debts that I owe to any manner of person shall be well and
truely paid
        I give and bequeath unto my loveing Wife ELIZABETH TUSSLEY all my land and
housing I now enjoy with all my goods and cattle, and hogges which I am possessed of
and in case of hir mortality then I give and bequeath my land with all my goods and
Cattle and hogges (which I am possessed of - marked out) unto my Son in Law GRIFFIN
CARTER and if it should please God to take him out of this life before he cometh to the
age of One and Twenty years then I give and bequeath my lands goods and Cattle unto
my loveing Freind Capt. JOHN HULL whom I make my Executor of this my Will
        In Witness whereof I have set my hand and Seale
in presence of FRANCIS STONE.   WILLIAM ✕ TUSSLEY Seale
     ROGER HULL. WILLIAM ⊕ WEBB
Recordatr Sexto die Aprilis 1673

   Wee the Subscribers doe heerby declare and testifie that we did see the within named
WILLIAM TUSSLEY sign seal & publish this within mentioned as his Last Will and Testament and that he was then in perfect mind and memory to the best of our Judgments
as Witness our hands this 5th day of March 1672/3
     ROGER HULL
     FRANCIS STONE
  Jurat in Cu Com Rappa 5 die Martii 1672/3

pp.   IN THE NAME OF GOD Amen this Eighth day of Februarie in the year of our Lord
133-   God one thousand Six hundred Seaventy Two I JOHN HARDESTY of the County of
134   Rappa in Virginia Planter being weake in body but of good and perfect mind &
        memory thanks bee given to Almighty God for the same considering with my
Self that nothing is more certain than death doe therefore make and ordaine this my
last Will and Testament in manner following
        First I give and bequeath my Soule into the hands of Almighty God my Creator
hoping to be saved onely by Jesus Christ my blessed Savioure and redeemer Next I commit my body to the Earth to have Christian buriall and for my Earthly Estate I give as
followeth

Item I give and bequeath unto my loveing Wife MARY HARDESTY all my personall Estate and likewise my Seate of land I bought of Mr. GEORGE PLEY to hir and hir heirs lawfully begotten for ever

Further in case my sd Wife bee with child now with eithr. boy or maide that then my Wife shall have only hir thirds and my sd Child shall have the other two thirds both of goods and lands but in case she is not with Child that then my sd Wife shall have all as aforesd my debts and funerall expences being first paide and further I doe make my sd Wife MARY HARDESTY my Sole Executrix of this my Last Will and Testamt. and doe revoake all other Wills and Testaments by me made by word of mouth or writeing

In Witness whereof I doe set my hand and seale the day and yeare above written
Test ROBERT PLEY,   JOHN HARDESTY   seale
    EDWARD ROWZIE
Recordatr Sexto die Aprilis 1673

  I the Subscribed doe heereby declare that I did see JOHN HARDESTY Signe seale and publish this within written Will and that he was in perfect Sence and memory at the time of makeing thereof
          EDWARD ROWZIE Juratus est 5 die Martii 1672/3

pp.   IN THE NAME OF GOD Amen I WILLIAM HODGKIN of Rappa in Virginia being
134-   bound for England and the dangers of the Sea to undergoe having my perfect
136   sence & memory doe by these presents renounce and make void all former Wills
       and Testaments by me made and doe make this my Last Will and Testament
    Imp. I give & bequeath my Soul to Almighty God which gave it me and my body to bee buried according to the Christian buriall and as for my temporall Estate I bequeath as followeth
    1st I give and bequeath unto my Kinsman SAMUEL PEACHY SENIOR two thousand pounds of tobacco in Cask to be paid by my Executors the next Crop after Administration
    It I give to his Eldest Sonne SAMUEL PEACHY my Godchild one Ewe and Lamb
    It I give and bequeath to his youngest Sonne WILLIAM PEACHY one three yeare old heiffer and one ewe and lamb
    It I give and bequeath to my Brother in Law HENRY SMITH my bay Mare
    It I give and bequeath unto my Servant JOHN BOOLES one Cow and Calfe out of my Stock
    It I give and bequeath unto Mr. THOMAS PEENIE the Colt of my bay Mare
    It I give and bequeath unto a MINISTER of my Executrix hir appointment five hundred pounds of tobacco to preach a Sermon in remembrance of me
    Lastly I give and bequeath unto my loving Wife PHEEBE HODGKIN all the remaindr. of my whole Estate in Virginia both personall and reall my debts being first paid and I doe appoint my Wife to bee my Executrix to see this my Will performed. In Witness to this my last Will and Testament I have hereunto set my hand & seale this 22 of March 1671/2
Witnesses RICHARD BRAY,   WILLIAM HODGKIN   Seale
          RALPH GRAYDON

  I RICHARD BRAY doe declare that I did see the abovementioned WILLIAM HODGKIN signe seale and publish this abovementioned as his last Will and Testament and that he was then in perfect mind and memory to the best of my Judgment as Witness my hand this 7th of May 1673

                                                    RICHARD BRAY

Juratus est in Cu Com Rappa 7 die May

pp.   IN THE NAME OF GOD Amen I ELIZABETH BUTLER of the Parish of Sittingbourne
136-   in the County of Rappa being in sound and perfect sence and memory doe make
143   and ordaine this my last Will and Testament revoaking and annihillating all
         other Wills and Codicells by me formerly made in manner and forme following
         Item I bequeath my Soul into the hands of Almighty God and my body to the
Earth from whence it was taken
         Item I give and bequeath unto my Sonne FRANCIS SLAUGHTER all the furniture
of my Chamber except a Chest of drawers which I give unto my Daughter SARAH to bee
delivered to hir at hir age of Seaventeene years or day of Marriage which shall first
happen and a close Stool to my Sonne JOHN CATLETT to be delivered to him when he goes
to housekeeping
         Item I give & bequeath unto my Sonne FRANCIS SLAUGHTER all the goods money
plate rings and Tobacco mentioned in an Account now in the hands of Mr. DANIEL
GAINES and one negro boy and an equall share of the Sheep pewter brasse and iron &
also a great Chair and small Couch and one Chest and such of the things in my house as
my Mother gave me by Will the same to bee delivered into his possession when he
comes to the age of Nineteen yeares and that he shall not dispose or sell the same without leave and consent of my Executor, and Overseers heereafter mentioned till he comes
to the age of one & twenty years
         Item I give and bequeath unto my Daughter ELIZABETH the bed & furniture as it
now is standing in the dining roome and the presse and cushion thereon the great
Looking Glasse and the Drawing Table and Turky Carpett and my Child bed linning
blanketts and fine baskett and my wedding ring and my biggest diamond ring my
gilded bodkin and my necklace with the biggest pearle and one small Bible a Silver
Sucking bottle & my small cabinett
         Item I give and bequeath unto my Daughter SARAH two of my biggest Stone
rings a small pearle necklace and a silver bodkin and my new trunck and the napkin
presse one small table and small Testament & a dram Cup my Wedding ring & ovall table
         Item I give and bequeath unto my Sonne JOHN one small diamond ring the mapp
in the dining roome, one rapier and one great Cutlash one paire of Silver buttons and
one paire of Silver buckles and the Antimonial Cupp
         Item I give & bequeath unto my Sonne WILLIAM one small Cutlash and a ring
with a Stone in it enamelled with blew and a Silver Seale
         Item I give and bequeath unto my two Daughters all my wearing Cloathes and
wearing linnen
         Item I give and bequeath unto my Sonne JOHN and Sonne WILLIAM all the
bookes mentioned in the Inventory equally between them according to their Fathers
Will
         Item I give and bequeath unto my two Sonnes JOHN & WILLIAM CATLETT and my
two Daughters all my plate except three spoones with their names on them to whom
they belong to bee equally devided between them
         Item I give and bequeath all my pewter brass linnen & other household stuff
unto my two Sonnes JOHN & WILLIAM and my two Daughters (except what is before bequeathed to my Sonne FRANCIS) with a bed furnished to each of my two Sones and my
Daughter SARAH (except two Suites of Damask which I give to my two Daughters) to bee
equally devided between my two Sonnes and two Daughters aforesd
         Item I give to each of my three Sonnes a Carbine
         Item I give and bequeath my gray mare with hir increase unto the aforesd
fower children of my deceased husband JOHN CATLETT

Item my will is that my two Daughter aforesd shall have delivered to them their former legacies at their day of marriage or at the years of Seventeene and likewise that my two Sonns JOHN and WILLIAM have theirs delivered when they come of age

Item I give and bequesth unto my Couzen WILLIAM UNDERWOOD the Elder one Stoned Colt which came of the Sorrell mare

Item I give and bequeath unto my Couzen HUMPHRY BOOTH the Chest with the goods in it which were my Mothers

Item I give & bequeath unto my Couzen CATHERINE BOOTH one Silver Candle Cupp which was hir Grandmothers and in case she dyes unto hir Bro. HUMPHREY

Item my will is that if my Son FRANCIS dye before he comes to age that my Children Surviving enjoy the whole Estate both formerly and now bequeathed unto him

Item my will is that if my Executor hereafter mentioned shall brake up house-keeping that then all my household stuff aforesd bequeath to my Children shall be well packed and locked up & kept from use and that the linnen and other things that are in the Cask & trunck be forthwith locked up till the time of their delivery and that all my Sonne FRANCIS his household stuff be likewise reserved and kept by it self

Item I give & bequeath to my Sister PEIRCE a mourning Ring of twenty shillings price in England

Item that if my Executor hereafter mentioned shall voluntarily surrender up the estate that then Mr. DANIEL GAINES if he hath the Children shall have the estate provided that he give good Security to keep the sd Estate entire and deliver the same in kind according to my Will and that this my Will bee by him in all respects performed as my Executor is bound to doe

Item my will is that my Executor supply what Tobaccoe shall be required for my Childrens Education now in England according to my Husbands Will and likewise that he make sufficient provision when they shall come from Schoole for their accomoda-tion and their bringing of them home to Virginia

Item my will is that all my wearing cloathes which last yeare I sent for as the profitt of my Tobaccoes bee upon the arrival of the same locked up in my Cask kept for & devided between my two Daughters and the rest my Executor to have for his house-hold use

And likewise what moneys shall remaine in Mr. JEFFRIES and Mr. MANFORDs hands in London be disbursed by them for a bed & furniture for my Son FRANCIS in lieu of one his Father in Law did owe him and two small Silver tankards (if it so holds out) to be added to the rest of the plate for the Children of my deceased Husband

Item my will is that the Childrens Estate be kept entire and not parted before their legacies given by me become due unto them and if the Court shall take my Chil-drens Estate out of my Executors hands that then my Children shall altogether be main-tained well educated & provided for by and with the profitt of their own estate and that my thirds and the profitts thereof shall remain in my Executors hands till they come of age

Item I do constitute and appoint my beloved Husband AMORY BUTLER Sole Exe-cutor of this my last Will & Testament and Guardian to my Children and my Cousen Captain THOMAS HAWKINS, my Bro. EDWARD ROWSEE and Mr. DANIEL GAINES Overseers of this my last Will & Testament provided that if my sd Executor do not Educate & keep them well that then Mr. DANIEL GAINES shall have Guardianship of my Children my sd Executor allowing him a sufficient maintenance for their well being and education according as my Overseers and Executor shall agree and if they do not what the Court shall determine for the same and if Mr. GAINES shall dye my desire is that my Cousen HAWKINS do take the Children upon the same terms and if my Executor shall imbezill the estate or forsake the Country then my will is that my Overseers shall call him to account and finding him delinquent my Executor shall be either bound to make good the same out of his own Estate or else yield it up to Mr. DANIEL GAINES the sd GAINES doing as before for the Security of the Estate

Item that my sd Executor doe purchase as soon as he can a negro man for my Sonne FRANCIS by or with the profitt of the Estate in lieu of one his Father in Law deceased did owe him

Item I give and bequeath of the Catle that were my Mothers and now in the keeping of THOMAS KIRK two of the female to my Sister PEIRCE hir children with their Increase for ever and also the other two of the female kind with their increase and eight steers to my Bro. BOOTHs Children, the sd Steers and encrease of the female to be disposed of by my Executor to purchase them a negro woman and the same to bee delivered to them with hir increase when they come of age and quality excepted

Item my will is that if the Estate of my Children shall bee taken out of my Executors hand within halfe a year after my decease and if my Executor be compelled to make good of the sd Estate what shall be falling short my Executor shall make good the same out of the encrease of the negroes that have bin since the same have bin committed to him the sd Increase to bee delivered to my Children in kind when they come of age, and if it shall not suffice then the same to bee made good out of my thirds or the profitts thereof as my Executor shall think best for my Children

Item I give and bequeath to my beloved Husband AMORY BUTLER a bed & furniture with a mourning ring of Twenty two shillings price in England

Item when my Executor shall have paid all my legacies that then if there be remaining any of my thirds in his hands he shall surrender up the same unto my Children the profitts thereof excepted

In witness whereof I have hereunto sett my hand & Seale the day & yeare above written

Signed sealed & declared to bee hir   ELIZABETH BUTLER   Seal
  last Will and Testament as Witness
    THOMAS LUCAS SENR.)   Sworne before me
       JOHN DAWSON)   JAMES KAY by order of Court
Juratus est in Cu Co Rappa 7 die May 1673
Probatr - Recordat x6 die June 1673

pp.   IN THE NAME OF GOD Amen I WILLIAM GRAY being Sick & weake but of perfect
143-   memory thanks to be God for it doe make ordaine constitute and appoint this to
145   bee by last Will and Testament revoaking and annulling all other Wills either
by word or writing by me formerly made and this only to bee and stand in full force & virtue and no other as in manner & form following

Imprs. I Surrender & give my Soul into the hands of the Almighty God my heavenly Father in pfect hope of pardon in and through the alone merritts of my dr Saviour & my body to be decently buried at the discreation of my Executor & Executrix hereafter named in assurance of ressurrection at the last day

Item I give and bequeath the tract of land I now live upon conteinging Seven hundred twenty & eight acres with the houses edifices thereunto belonging unto my Sonnes JOHN GRAY and WARWICK GRAY equally to be devided between them to them & their heirs for ever

Item I give unto my Sons WILLIAM GRAY & ABNER GRAY my tract of land conteining four hundred Sixty one acres adjoyning to OCCUPACY RUN equally to bee devided between them to them and their heirs for ever and if it should please God that if either of my Sons dye before they come to be of age that then that moyety or half of land to return to the Survivor which did belong to him

    Item my will is that my Executor & my Executrix or either of them shall buy a young Mare for my Sons in Law TOBY and THOMAS INGRAM between this and the last of Aprill which shall be in the year of our Lord 1675 to belong to the sd TOBY & THOMAS INGRAM and theire heirs for ever with the increase of the sd Mare

    Item I give to my Son ABNER aforesd a black Mare with all hir increase which was purchased with a Gift to him from Mr. ABERNETHY

    Item I give my Daughter MARY GRAY the first mare Colt that my own Mare brings

    Item I give to my Grandchild ELIZABETH BOWLER a Cow called Mad Buck

    Item I make ordaine and appoint my Son in Law JAMES BOWLER and my beloved Wife MAUDLIN GRAY Executor & Executrix of this my Will

    In Witness whereof I have heereunto set my hand & Seale the 20th of July 1673 in presence of us WARWICK CAMMOCK,

    FRANCIS F STERNE   WILLIAM G GRAY   Seal

FRANCIS STERNE aged about thirty five years & WARWICK CAMMOCK aged 37 years deposed & say that this above written is the last Will & Testament of WILLIAM GRAY and that he was in perfect sence & memory at the making thereof & that they saw him Sign & seal the same

                              WARWICK CAMMOCK
                              FRANCIS F STERNE

Jurati in Cu Com Rappa 3 die 7bris 1673
  et Recordatr 8 die xbris 1673

Pages 146-148 Repeat of WILLIAM GRAY's Will

pp.   THE LAST WILL & TESTAMENT of CORNELIUS SWELLIVANT made December 1672
148-   In the Name of God Amen first I give freely unto JOHN BURRIDG all my land
149   during his life and one feather bed & one chest one trunck & all my working
        tools and all my household goods belonging to me and my boate

    Item I give unto THOMAS NORTON Sonne to PATRICK NORTON three hundred & fifty acres of land on the upper side of the Divident and after the decease of THOMAS NORTON & JOHN BURRIDGE the land to fall to PATRICK NORTON

    Item unto JOHN KELLY Sonne of MATHEW KELLY I give one hundred Seaventy five acres joyning upon the land that the sd MATHEW KELLY now liveth on in the mean time MATHEW KELLy may put it to what use he please and after the decease of JOHN KELLy the land to fall to MATHEW KELLY his Father

    Item what Cattle the sd JOHN BURRIDGE shall receive of CORNELIUS SULLIVANT he to leave so many in kind to THOMAS NORTON

    Item to JOHN DOWTY I give one Dowlas Shirt one pair of kersey breeches and one Coate and three pewter dishes

    Item to PATRICK NORTON I give one hanger

Test WILLIAM MAJOR,   CORNELIUS SWELLIVANT
    JOHN F O ORGILL

Both which did in open Court Sware
the 19th day of November 1673 that they saw CORNELIUS SWELLIVANT sign this Will & that it was his last Will & Testament upon which a Probat was graunted to PATRICK NORTON, JOHN BURRIDG not proving the same

               Test EDMD CRASK ClCur

pp.   IN THE NAME OF GOD Amen I HENRY PETERS being Sick & weake but of sound &
149-   perfect memory thankes bee to God for it do make ordain Constitute & appoint
151   this to bee my last Will & Testament revoaking & disannulling all other Will or
       Wills either verbal or otherwise by me formerly made

       Imp. I Surrender my Soul into the hands of Almighty God my Saviour & Re-
deemer and for the worldly goods which it hath pleased God to bestow upon me I give &
dispose as followeth

       Item I give & bequeath the two Girles ELIZABETH WALKER & MARY PETERS to
my beloved Wife and at their Mothers decease that JOHN SMITH should not meddle with
them so likewise it is my will & desire

       Item I give & bequeath unto JAMES ALLEN my Wifes Sonne three hundred acres
of land lying near PEUMONDSON to bee laid out together to him & his heires for ever

       Item I give & bequeath to my Daughter ELIZABETH WALKER two Cowes and a
Mare of a year or two years old to bee paid hir the day of hir Marriage

       Item I give & bequeath all the rest of my Estate both reall & personall to my well
beloved Wife JANE PETERS & to my Daughter MARY PETERS to be devided equally
between them by my loving Freinds Mr. LAURENCE WASHINGTON, JOHN MEADER,
FRANCIS STERNE & WARWICK CAMMOCK within three weekes or thereabts. after my decease and my request to them is that they would devide it as equally as they can to the
best of their Judgments because my will is that their bee no appraisment made of any
part of my Estate also I make constitute and appoint my well beloved Wife JANE PETERS
the Sole Executrix of this my Will
in presence of us Januarie the 30th 1673
         PETER DUNNIVAN.   Signum HENRY PETERS   Seale
         JOHN GIBSON, WARWICK CAMMOCK

         An Addition to the Will of HENRY PETERS within mentioned
                          January the 30th 1673/4
I HENRY PETERS do hereby will and desire that in case my beloved Wife JANE PETERS
shall depart this life before my Daughters ELIZABETH WALKER & MARY PETERS come to
be of age then DANIEL GAINES & WARWICK CAMMOCK do take charge of them & their
Estate & if the sd GAINES & CAMMOCK dye in the mean time the Survivor is heereby
impowered to choose an other. Witness my hand & Seale the day and year above written
in presence of us PETER DUNNIVAN.   Signum   HENRY ✝ PETERS   seale
         JOHN GIBSON

       Wee whose names are subscribed do aver upon our Oaths that this above & within writ-
ten Will was the last Will and Testament of HENRY PETERS and that he was in perfect
sence & memory to the best of our Judgments at the time of the making thereof
                                                WARWICK CAMMOCK
                                                PETER DUNNIVAN
                                                JOHN GIBSON
Jurati in Cu Com Rappa 4 die Martii
A Probate heereon is granted to JANE PETERS

pp.   IN THE NAME OF GOD Amen I THOMAS LUCAS the Elder of the Parish of Sitting-
152-   bourne in the County of Rappa being in good health and sound memory but
154   aged & not knowing how soone and after what manner it may please God to take
       me out of this world do make and ordaine this my Last Will and Testament in
manner & form following & revoaking heereby all other Wills & Codicills by me formerly made the fourteenth day of October One thousand Six hundred Sixty & nine

Imprs. I bequeath my Soul into the hands of Almighty God my Creator & Redeemer and my body to the Earth from whence it was taken trusting thro the mercy of God & the merritts & mediation of Jesus Christ to rise again at the last day into eternall life

Item I give & bequeath unto my Son in Law JOHN CATLETT ten shillings

Item I give & bequeath unto my Grandchild MARY HAWKINS one young heiffer with a Cow Calfe & all their female increase to bee delivered by my Executors hereafter named unto my Sonne HAWKINS aforesd to keep for hir within one year after my decease and the male increase to himself for his charge and care in keeping them and he the sd Cattel and female increase to deliver to hir at hir age of one & twenty years or day of Marriage which shall first happen

Item I give & bequeath unto my Son THOMAS LUCAS all my lands tenemts. & the hereditaments with the appurtenaces to him and his heirs for ever

Item all the residue of my goods & chattels my debts & legacies being paid I give and bequeath unto my Son THOMAS LUCAS aforesd whom I make sole Executor of this my last Will & Testament Witness my hand & Seale

in presence of EDMUND DOBSON,   THOMAS LUCAS SENR.   Seale
    RICHARD R WEST

An Addition to the Last Will & Testament of THOMAS LUCAS SENR. made the 24th of March 1673

Item my will is that my Executor do in due and convenient time after my decease pay and satisfie all my just debts & in particular my will is that my loving Sister in Law Mrs. MARGARET PLAMMER bee paid as soon as may bee after my decease Five pounds Sterling or the just value thereof in Sweet Scented tobacco

It I give & bequeath unto my Loving Son in Law THOMAS HAWKINS one thousand pounds of tobo. to be paid in two years after my decease

Item I give and bequeath unto my loving Friend DANIEL GAINES ten Shillings Sterling

Item my will & desire is that my Son in Law THOMAS HAWKINS be aiding & assisting to my Sonn & Execu(blot) THOMAS LUCAS in what he shall reasonably require of him either for advice or otherwise to the truth whereof I have heereunto sett my hand & Seale the day & year abovesd

Signed sealed & declared   THOMAS LUCAS SENR.   Seale
    to bee a Codicill of my Last Will
    & Testamt. in presence of THOMAS HAWKINS,
        DANIEL D S: SHIPHY

Wee the Subscribers do aver upon our Oaths that this within written Will with the Codicell annexed was the last Will and Testamt. of Mr. THOMAS LUCAS and that at the signing & sealing thereof he was in perfect sence & memory to the best of our Judgments

                    THOMAS HAWKINS
                    DANIEL b:J:SHIPHY
                    RICHARD R WEST

Juratus as to the Will May the 27th 1674
Jurati THOMAS HAWKINS & DANIEL SHIPHY to the Will & Codicil May the 27th 1674
Probate hereon is granted
Recordatr x5 die Junii 1674

pp.   IN THE NAME OF GOD Amen I RALPH WARRINER being Sick in body but of per-
155-   fect mind & memory praised bee God for the same make and ordain this my
156   last Will and Testament in manner and forme as followeth my body I desire to

bee buried at home with or near my Father & Mother at the discretion of THOMAS GOULDMAN

Item I give unto FRANCES KEYE my Cow Squirrell as useth Colo. VASSELLs old Plantacon that was

Item I give my horse to WILLIAM DYER

Item I give all the tobo. that belongeth to me out of the Cropp or is otherwise properly due to me unto my Guardian THOMAS GOULDMAN he laying out of the same for my Sisters particular use five hundred out of the same in necessarys as he shall think fitting

Item I give unto my Sister three young black Cows & one Steere three years old or thereabts. and one Bull of two years old & one yearling heiffer and also two Sowes that I have on the Plantation and for confirmation hereof I hereunto set my hand & Seale this 7th day of March Ano 1673

in presence of us ROBERT ↰ PARKER,   RALPH ↰ WARRINER Seale
                    WILLIAM ✕ DYER

Wee the Subscribed do aver upon our Oaths that this within written is the last Will & Testament of RALPH WARRINER deceased and that he was in perfect sence and memory to the best of our Judgments

                              ROBERT ↰ PARKER
                              WILL + DIER

Recordatr Test EDM CRASE Cl Cur
Jurati in Cl Com Rappa xx7 die May 1674

pp   THIS BEING my Last Will & Testament I doe heereby commit my Soul to God and
156-   my Body to the Earth. This my will & desire is that my three hundred acres of
157   land shall be at my Landladys SARAH BOWYERS dispose to doe what she think fitt
         to sell or otherwise and if the sd SARAH BOWYER die without any Will then the sd
Three hundred acres of land to bee devided between SAMUEL FLOOD & BRIDGETT ESSEX the Daughter of JOHN ESSEX and further my Will is that the sd BRIDGET ESSEX shall have one heiffer about two years & a half old and hir increase for ever and also I give one Steere about the same age to SAMUEL FLOOD. And Further my will is that my Landlady SARAH BOWYERS shall have all the rest of my Cattel & hogges to doe what she please either to sell or otherways what she shall think fitt as Witness my hand & Seale this 18th day of April of our Lord God 1673
Test JOSHUA LAWSON,   JOHN ⫟ P: PACKSTON
     THOMAS ✕ WARRING

JOSHUA LAWSON averred in open Court upon his Oath that this above written was the last Will & Testamt. of JOHN PAXTON deceased & that he was in prfect sence & memory to the best of his Judgment at the signing & sealing thereof
                                    JOSHUA LAWSON

Jurati est LAWSON in Cu Com Rappa xx7 die Maii 1674

pp.   IN THE NAME OF GOD Amen I GEORGE MOTT of the Pish of Sittingbourne in the
157-   County of Rappa Planter being Sick & Weake of body but in perfect sence &
161   memory blessed be God do make my last Will & Testament in manner & form
         following first I commit my Soul to God that gave it me and my body to the Earth
to bee decently buried at the discretion of my Surviving Freinds and for what part of the Devident of land on the North side of RAPPA RIVER granted to my Bror. JOHN MOTT and I by Patent dated at JAMES CITY the Seventeenth of October 1670 my will is that my

well beloved Wife ELIZABETH MOTT shall enjoy one third thereof during hir naturall life and that the land be equally divided among my Children Vizt. ELIZABETH, MARGARET, ANNE and ELLEN and if it shall happen that my Wife bee with Child at my death and the Child live that it shall have an equall part with the rest but if it be a Son my will is that if any one of my daughters abovesd depart this life before she come to age or married that then the Son shall enjoy hir part of the land and in case more of my Children dye my will is that the Survivors bee joynt heirs. Then as for my personal estate my will is that my well beloved Wife have and enjoy one third part thereof for ever to bee at hir disposall and the other two thirds to be equally divided among the Children to bee delivered in kind as in respect of age and quality either when they marry or come to the age of Seventeen years And Whereas my Bro: and I have joyntly given to the Children some certain Sheep and Cattle my desire is that they be distinguist by a marke and that they with their increase bee by my Wife improved to the Childrens best advantage. And I do make and appoint my well beloved Wife to bee my sole Executrix of this my Last Will and Testament and I doe desire that my well beloved Bror. JOHN MOTT would bee assistant to hir in the management of the Estate and for the pformance thereof my desire is that an Inventorie bee taken of all the psonall Estate appertaining to my Bror. and I and that noe division be made thereof but that they would live together upon the Plantacon with the estate joyntly as my Bror. and I formerly have done onely dividing the Cropp yearly & each to have the disposall of theire part at their own discretion but if it should happen that any inconvenience should arise that they shall see cause to divide the estate and live apart that then my Brother shall have one half of the profitts of the Orchard during his life and I do further give liberty to my Executrix and my Bror. to sell one thousand acres of the devident of land abovesd before the Division thereof betwixt them and to devide the produce thereof betwixt them equally and the remaidner of the land to be equally divided betwixt my Bror. and my Children and Whereas there is an Instrument of Writing made betwixt my Bror. and I under our hands & Seals on purpose to destroy joyntenancie betwixt us bearing date the 10th of October 1671 wherein mention is also made of certain parcells of land conveyed and to bee conveyed to severall persons as allso two thousand acres of land sould, & acknowledged in Court to Mr. WILLIAM THORNTON therefore it is my will that if my Executrix or any of my Children shall act or do anything contrary to the true intent & meaning of our severall agreements with these parties that then the damages arising thereby shall be made good out of their or any of their part of my estate

I do likewise constitute and appoint my well beloved Wife ELIZABETH MOTT to be my Executrix of the last Will and Testament of Mr. SOLOMON MARTIN and do desire that my said Wife having the consent of my Bror. JOHN MOTT (if living) to dispose of the increase of the estate given to my Children by the sd SOLOMON MARTIN as also the estate abovesd already in their possession to the use and benefitt of my Children & to do no other end or purpose And I do by this Will & Testament revoake all other Wills & Testaments. As Witness my hand & Seal this last day of March 1674

Test JAMES HARRISON   GEORGE MOTT   Seal
     JOHN BOWSIER, HENRY ✝ HACKREY

Wee the Subscribers doe averr and upon our Oaths that this within written was the last Will & Testament of Mr. GEORGE MOTT and that he was in pfect sence & memory to the best of our Judgments at the signing & sealing thereof

                                         JAMES HARRISON
                                         HENRY ✝ HACKREY

A probat hereon is granted to Mrs. ELIZABETH MOTT his relict
Jurati in Cu Com Rappa xx7 die May 1674

pp.   IN THE NAME OF GOD Amen the Last Will & Testament of PETER ELDER being in
161-   pfect sence & memory I do bequeath my Soul to God and my body to the earth
162   Item I doe bequeath my Sonn PETER ELDER unto Mr. RICHARD PEACOCK he
being my Sons Godfather whom I have made choice of above all others and as
for what Stock of Cattle I have I give to my Son PETER and a heifer of three years old
due by Bill from JOHN ARNOLD due to bee paid according to Bill, And as for what stock of
Cattle I give to my Son PETER Mr. PEACOCK to have the benefitt of them untill my Sonn
comes to bee one and Twenty years of age Mr. PEACOCK to have the male and my Sonne
the Female and as for my Plantation and all moveable goods else Mr. PEACOCK to take
into his Custody untill the boy comes to bee one & twenty. In this I appoint my loving
Friend Mr. RICHARD PEACOCK to bee my Executor in full in whole And to the true performance of this my last Will and Testament I sett my hand & Seale this 28th of Aprill
1674
in presence of us GEORGE HOWELL,   PETER E ELDER   Seale
        RICHARD APPBLEBEE his ℛℳmarke

  Wee GEORGE HOWELL and RICHARD APPLEBEE doe declare that wee did see the within
menconed PETER ELDER sign seale and publish this within menconed to bee his last Will
& Testament and that he was then in pfect mind & memory to the best of our Judgmts.
As Witness our hands this 5th of August 1674
                                        GEORGE HOWELL
                                        RICHARD ℛℳAPPLEBEE
Jurati in Co Com Rappa 5 die Augusti 1674
Probatr & recordatr   Test EDMD. CRASK

pp.   IN THE NAME OF GOD Amen I JOHN DREWITT Sick of body but in perfect sence and
163-   memory bequeath my body to the ground and my Soul to God that gave it in sure
164   and certain hope of the resurrection of both Body & Soul at the last day
        I doe give to ELIZABETH SAXON one yearling heiffer called by the name of
Browning and to ANNE SAXON Daughter the sd JOHN SAXON I do give one Cow Calfe not
yet marked the remaining part of my estate I give RICHARD GLOVER makeing him the
sd RICHARD GLOVER full & whole Executor of this my last Will & Testament. As Witness
my hand & Seale this 28th day of July 1674
Test THO: FRESHWATER,   JOHN ℋℋ DRUIT   Seale
        JOHN ⅄ JONES, JOHN SAXON
  I doe declare that I did see the above mentioned JOHN DRUIT sign seale & publish this
as his last Will and Testament as Witness my hand this 5th of August 1674 & that he was
in perfect mind & memory to the best of my Judgment
                                        THO: FRESHWATER

  I JOHN JONES doe declare that I did see the above mentioned JOHN DRUIT sign seale &
publish the above mentioned to bee his last Will & Testament and that he was in pfect
mind & memory to the best of my Judgment. As Witness my hand this 5th of August
1674
                                        JOHN ⅄ JONES
Jurati in Cu Com Rappa 5 die Augusti 1674
Probate & recordatr.

pp.   IN THE NAME OF GOD AMEN the last Will & Testament of BARBARY BILLINGTON
164-   being sick & weake in body but of perfect mind & memory
166   Imp. I bequeath my Soul to Almighty God that gave it where through the

merritts of Christ Jesus my Saviour I hope to inherit eternall life my body I bequeath to my Mother earth to bee decently buried as for my worldly Estate I give as
followeth Viz.

    Item I give to my Daughter JANE one pair of large andirons

    Item I give to my Daughter BARBARY one large Copper Kettle

    Item All the rest of my Estate moveables and unmoveables Chattels Servants
Debts and all worldly Estate belonging unto me my just debts being first satisfyed I give
and bequeath to bee equally devided amongst my Children ELISHA RUSSELL, LUKE
BILLINGTON, ELIZABETH BILLINGTON, JANE and BARBARY and in case of the mortality
of any of them before they attain to their lawfull ages my desire is that their part be
equally devided amongst the Surviveing Children and doe ordaine and appoint my
Daughter ALISHA RUSSELL and LUKE BILLINGTON my Sone my full and Sole Executors of
this my last Will & Testament desiring my loving Friends Mr. ROBERT BAYLY, Mr.
HENRY CLERK & Mr. SAMUEL PEACHY to be Overseers of my sd Children and their estate
untill they attaine to their respective ages and in case any difference should happen
among my sd Children in the Division of their Legacies or the Explanation of this my
Intent in my Will and to avoid all Law suits and expences that may happen thereby I
refer and leave it totally and fully to the determinations of my aforesaid Overseers.

    In Witness whereof I have set my hand & Seale this 7th day of August Ano 1674
in presence of us JNO. STONE,   BARBARY ₿: ₿:BILLINGTON Seale
    HENRY WILSON
      NATHANIEL RICHARDSON

  Mr. HENRY WILLSON aged forty six years or thereabouts and NATHANIEL RICHARDSON
aged Twenty eight years or thereabouts depose & say that they did see Mrs. BARBARY
BILLINGTON Sign seale & publish this within written as hir last Will and Testament &
she was in perfect sence & memory to the best of their Judgments at the signing
thereof   HENRY WILSON
                             NATHANIEL RICHARDSON

Jurati in Cu Com Rappa xxi die Octob 1674
A probat hereon was granted to hir Executors

pp.   THE DEPOSITION of JOHN STRINGER aged 30 years or thereabts. Sworn & Examined
166-   Saith
167   That WILLIAM STOAKES lying sick at yr deponts. house he your deponent being
       to goe from home asked the sd STOAKES if it pleased God to take him out of this
world before my return how will you dispose of your Bills the sd STOAKES replyed unto
my Cozen SAMUEL PARRY & further saith not
Juratur Coram nobis   JOHN ∫ STRINGER
    ROBERT ABRAHALL,
      ROGER MALLARY
Recordatr x die 9bris 1674

pp.   THE LAST WILL & TESTAMENT of THOMAS MADDISON made October the 19th 1674
167-   In the Name of God Amen I THOS. MADDISON being very sick & weake yet of
169   perfect sence and memory doe give and bequeath my Soul to God that gave it me
      and my body to the dust from whence it came

    Imprimis I THOMAS MADDISON doe allso give & bequeath unto CATHERINE
MADDISON my Wife all my moveable goods within dore and without that are mine or
that belongeth or appertaineth to me the sd THOMAS MADDISON

    I doe also give and bequeath unto the sd KATHARINE MADDISON my Wife all Catle in General both young and old and hoggs likewise both young & old that are runing within my Plantation or without or wheresoever else that belongeth or appertaineth properly unto me the sd THOMAS MADDISON furthermore I the sd THOMAS MADDISON doe leave my Plantation and all my land to cleere and discharge all my debts which I owe onely three hundred acres which I sould to RICHARD WHITE and a parcell of land which I sould to RICHARD SIMMS and all the rest of my land I doe leave to discharge my debts which belong to a Patent or Pattents and if there bee anything left over and above more then shall pay my debts then it shall return to KATHARINE MADDISON my Wife Furthermore I doe leave my loving Friends and Neighbours RICHARD WHITE and THOMAS BRYANT Executors of this my Will and Testament and to bee assistant to KATHA-REINE MADDISON my Wife, And I doe allso give my long Gun to THOMAS BRYANT and my Short Gun to RICHARD WHITE. I do also give to my Godchild REBECKA PETTIE the Daughter of ROBERT PETTIE one heiffer of two years old furthermore I do give and leave unto KATHARINE MADDISON my Wife my mony which I have in England with my Bror. LEONARD MADDISON which is the sume of Seaventy pounds Sterling and unto this my Last Will and Testament I have hereunto sett my hand & seale

Test PETER CALVIN.   THO: MADDISON   Seale
    JOHN BIFOREST

  PETER CALVIN & JOHN BIFOREST do declare that this within written is the last Will & Testament of THOMAS MADDISON deceased and that they did see him sign & seale this as his last Will & Testament and that he was in pfect sence & memory to the best of their Judgment

PETER CALVIN
JOHN BIFORREST

Jurati in Cu com Rappa 4 die 9bris 1674
A probate herein is granted to Coll. WILLM. TRAVERS in the behalfe of ANNE MADDISON by order of this Court

p   BY THE NAME OF GOD I ELIAS BLAKE being Sick in body but of perfect mind and
170   memory make this my last Will & Testament I give my Soul to God and my body to
      the Earth to be buried at the discretion of HENRY MOUNCASTER and for my
worldly goods I bequeath as follows
    Item I give unto my Brother WALTER BLAKE my Mare finally I give and bequeath all the residue of my Estate to HENRY MONCASTER who I make my Sole Executor of this my last Will and Testament and for confirmation hereof I heerunto set my hand & seale this Eleventh day of June 1674

Signed, sealed & publised and   ELIAS BLAKE   Seale
  declared as his Last Will and Testament
in presence of us JOHN Ꝺ GOUDG,
    ELIZABETH O CATLETT

  Wee the Subscribers do declare upon or. oaths that this within written was the Last Will and Testament of ELIAS BLAKE and that he was in perfect sence and memory at the signing thereof to the best of our Judgments

JOHN GOUDG
Jurati in Com Rappa 6 die January 1674   ELIZABETH CATLET
Probatr et recordatr

pp.   IN THE NAME OF GOD Amen I JOHN BOLLIN being Sick in body but of sound and
171-   perfect memory do make this my last Will and Testament in manner following
172   Item I doe give and bequeath my Soul to Almighty God which gave it to me in
         hopes of a resurrection at the last day and my body to the burying of my dearest
friends
         I doe give & bequeath all my land unto MATHEW HARROD and her heirs after the
death of my Mother to MARTHA HARROD & her heirs forever. I doe give unto PETER
HAROD one yearling heifer and her increase for ever. I do give and bequeath all my
Cattle unto me deare Mother making her my lawfull Executrix this being my last Will
and Testament. As Witness my hand & seale this 27th of January in the year of our Lord
1674
in presence of us RICHARD ꝛ KING   JOHN + BULLINS   Seale
         THOMAS ⊥⊥ HINES

RICHARD KING aged abt. forty years depose and say that this above written was the
Last Will & Testamt. of JOHN BULLIN deced and that he was in pfect sence and memory to
the best of his Judgmt. at the signing and sealing thereof
                                        RICHARD ꝛ KING

THOMAS HINES aged twenty two years or thereabts. depose & say the same with the
former Evidence RICHARD KING
                                        THOMAS ⟂ HINES

Jurati in Cur Com Rappa 5 die May 1675
Probat hereon is granted

pp.   IN THE NAME OF GOD Amen I JOHN SPEEDE of the Parish of Sittingbourn in the
172-   Countie of Rappa being very weake & sick in body but of good and perfect
173   memory God be praised therefore I doe make & ordain this my last Will and
         Testament in manner & form following this Aprill the 18th day 1675
         Imprimis I bequeath my Soul into the hands of Almighty God my Creator & Re-
deemer trusting through the merritts & mediation of Jesus Christ to raise my body from
the earth from whence it was taken unto eternall life
         Item after my debts are truely & honestly paid a decent funerall to be made for
the accomodation of my Neighbours & Friends I doe give unto SARAH ALLEN two Cows
in the first place this prsent year and to enjoy them forever
         it is my will that a Cow Calfe should be given from one of the abovesd Cows this
next year unto WILLIAM THORPE and then my reall and personall Estate to be devided
between JOHN EAVENS and SARAH ALLEN equally. In Witness whereof I have heereunto set my hand & seale the day and year above written
Test PETER CORNWELL   JOHN I S SPEEDE   Seale
         FRANCIS F JENKINS

PETER CORNWELL aged 41 years or thereabts. depose and say that this above written
was the last Will and Testament of JOHN SPEEDE deceased and that he was in perfect
sence & memory to the best of his Judgment at the signing & sealing thereof.
                                        PETER CORNWELL

FRANCIS JENNING aged 27 yeares or thereabouts depose & say that he attested this
above written at the reqest of JOHN SPEEDE.
                                        FRANCIS F E JENNINGS

Jurantr in Cur Com Rappa 5 die May 1675
A Probat hereon is granted to MARTIN JOHNSON
in behalf of JNO. EVANS

pp.   IN THE NAME OF GOD Amen I RICHARD LOES of the County of Rappa in Virginia
174   being at prsent weak of body but in sound & perfect mind & memory praised be
176   God for it doe by these prsents renounceing all my former wills and testaments
make this my last Will & Testament in manner & form following

   Imprimis I bequeath my Soul to God my Creator who gave it me my body to
Christian buriall hoping through the merritts of Jesus Christ my only Saviour & Redeemer of a joyfull resurrection and all that Estate that it hath pleased God of his mercy
to bestow upon me I give & bequeath in manner and form as followeth

   Item I give & bequeath unto my Son in Law JAMES TACKET all the estate I have
in Maryland both Tobo. goods debts & otherwise and whereas I did Ship home for LIME
fifty hhds of Tobo. out of MARYLAND and consigned them unto WALTER TUCKER Merchant in LIME I also give & bequeath unto my sd Son JAMES TACKETT the full produce of
the sd fifty hogsheads unto him & his heirs forever

   Item I give & bequeath unto my Son in Law JAMES TACKETT the one halfe part
of the Stock of Cattle horses & mares that I am now possessed with & two Christian Servants for the full time they have to serve at their comming into this Country to be delivered him the next Shipping one fowling gun one pot two pewter dishes & two basons
& all the pewter which was his Mothers decd. I also ordain that my sd Son JAMES
TACKETT & Servants to have ground to worke on & houseroom to cure there cropps & for
their accommodation upon the plantacon whereon I now live for and during the space
of time of four yeares next ensuing after my death & to have free priviledge to grind
his Corne at my Mill toll free during his life or the time of his abode in this River

   Item I give & bequeath unto my Son in Law Mr. HENRY WILLIAMSON all my
lands lying in NIMCOCK in RAPPA RIVER which I formerly purchased of RICHARD
BENNETT & HENRY CORBIN Esqr. unto him the sd WILLIAMSON & his heirs forever

   Item I give & bequeath unto my sd Son in Law Mr. HENRY WILLIAMSON all the
rest of my personall Estate negroes Indians Mullattoes horses mares cattle moneys & all
other my Estate of wt. nature or kind soever here in this Country or elsewhere unto
him the sd WILLIAMSON & his heirs for ever and I do hereby ordain & appoint my said
Son in Law Mr. HENRY WILLIAMSON my Sole & absolute Executor of this my Last Will &
Testament willing him to pay all my debts & legacies above menconed

   In Witness whereof I have hereunto set my hand & seale this two & twentieth
day of Aprill 1675
Signed & sealed
in presence of MARY + HODGES.   RICHARD LOES   Seale
   RICHARD GRIMSTED. EDWARD THOMAS

   EDWARD THOMAS aged 32 yeares or thereabts. & RICHARD GRIMSTED aged 28 years or
thereabouts depose & say they did see Mr.RICHARD LOES abovemenconed signe Seale &
publish this above written as his last Will & Testament & that he was in perfect sence &
memory at the signing thereof to the best of their Judgments
                                             EDWARD THOMAS
                                             RICHARD GRIMSTED
   Proabtr p Sacramcutum EDWARD THOMAS & RICHARD GRIMSTED in Cur Com Rappa
7 die July 1675

pp.   THOMAS ERWIN aged 46 yeares or thereabouts Sworn saith that on or about the
177-   beginning of March last past this Deponent being at the house & plantacon
178   called ISLAND where JOHN RUSSELL then lived and the sd RUSSELL being at that
        prsent deprived of his Speech but according to my Judgment in perfect Sence
and memory did first according to this Deponts. understanding make signes to WILLIAM
SERJEANT to follow him the sd RUSSELL they went into a litle Shed and the sd RUSSELL
took two pewter dishes in his hand & made signes to his Sonne to give him one of the sd
Dishes and according to this Deponents understanding the sd RUSSELL made signe to
give the other Dish to his Daughter & coming out of the sd Shed went & opened a Small
box & tooke out two Silver Spoones & delivered the one of the sd Spoones to his aforesd
Son & the other Spoone according to this Deponents understanding the sd RUSSELL
made signes to give to his aforesd Daughter and afterwards the sd RUSSELL took out a
small box of which he took one Gold ring & one Silver seale & delivered the same to
WILLIAM SERJEANT and sd SERJEANT saying to the sd RUSSELL what to me the sd RUS-
SELL made signe to the Contrary, then the sd SERJEANT said to the sd RUSSELL what to
my Wife the sd RUSSELL then made Signes according to this Deponents understanding
that he did give the same to the sd SERJEANTs Wife after all which signes the sd RUS-
SELL put up the severall things above mentioned in the respective places where there
were And there they continued till the sd RUSSELLs decease to the best of this Deponents Judgment & farther saith not May the 17th 1675
Juratr Coram me Ano x die   THOMAS ERWIN
        WILLIAM MOSELEY
Probatr Sacrament THOM. ERWIN in Cur Com Rappa 7 die July 1675

pp   TO ALL XPIAN PEOPLE to whome these prsents may or shall hereafter conforme
178-   Know Yee that I QUINTILLIAN SHEERMAN being Sick & weak in body but in good
180   & perfect memory doe make this my last Will and Testament
        Imprimis my Soule I commend to God my make & Jesus Christ my Redeemer my
body to be Christian like buried and for the rest of my Estate wch it have pleased God to
give me I bestoweth as followeth
        Item I do give unto my Son QUINTILLIAN SHERMAN One hundred acres of land
wch land make all the clear ground orchard & all thereabout it, & one hundred acres of
woodland ground
        I do give unto my Son MARTIN SHERMAN the same soe equally to be devided as it
may not prvidus on the other Senr.
        I do give unto my daughter ANNE SHERMAN two Cowes by name Starr & Cherry
with their increase & for ever
        thirdly I doe give & bequeath unto my Son QUINTILLIAN One Cow by name Lilley
with her increase for ever & further it is my will & desire three yeares hence that my
Son QUINTILLIAN & my Daughter ANN give my Son MARTIN each of them a heiffer
apiece out of the increase of the Cows abovesd & further I do give my Son QUINTILLIAN
my Gun and for all the rest of my Estate that I have I doe freely give & bequeath it unto
my beloved Wife JANE SHERMAN the same to be at her own disposing
        In Witness hereof I have hereunto set my hand & Seale this 15th day of May in
the year of our Lord 1675
in presence of us RICHARD DUDLEY,   QUINTILLIAN X SHERMAN
        HENRY TILLEREY

        Wee the Subscribers do declare that wee did see the within menconed QUINTILLIAN
SHERMAN Signe Seale & publish this within menconed as his last Will & Testament &

that then he was in pfect sence & memory to the best of our Judgments as Witness our hands this 1st day of September 1675

RICHARD DUDLEY
HENRY TILLERY

Probatr p Sacramentum RICHARDI DUDLEY & HENRI TILLERY pmo die Sept 1675

pp.   IN THE NAME OF GOD Amen I THOMAS COOPER of Rappa. County being Sick in
180-   body but Sound in mind & of perfect memory do commit my Soul to Almighty God
182   that gave it me & do delcare this to be my last Will & Testament & that all my
        Estate shall be disposed of as is hereafter menconed

First my will is that my body may be decently buried by my Wife in the PISCA-TAWAY CHURCH YARD

Item I give & bequeath unto JOHN JONES the Eldest Son of RICHARD JONES deceased all the devident of land upon which my dwelling house now standeth on soe farr as the branch which leads to THOMAS HARPER for ever

Item I give unto RICHARD JONES another Son of RICHARD JONES aforesd all that devident of land beyond the sd Branch

Item I give & bequeath unto DOROTHY PETTY a red Cow known by the name of Browning

Item I give & bequeath unto DENNIS CONNIERS my Stuffe Coate and my large drawers

Item I give & bequeath all the rest of my wearing Cloaths to my Servant THOMAS

Item I give & bequeath unto JOHN SOPER my Gun which is now in my dwelling house

Item I give & bequeath unto JANE JONES Daughtr. of RICHARD JONES decd. aforesd one mare foale which now runeth by the old Mares side wth the sd Colts increase for ever

Item my will is that all my just debts due from me to any person be duely & truely satisfyed in the first place

Item I declare and make AVIS JONES Widw. my whole & sole Executrix & after that she hath satisfied the foremenconed prmises do give & bequeath unto her all my household goods & Stock of what nature or kind soever & all debts due to me and my Servants and my will is that my Executrix shall possess and enjoy the aforesd devidents of land during her naturall life and after her decease to return as abovesd

Item I declare this to be my last Will and Testament revoaking all former wills in Testimonie whereof I have hereunto set my hand & Seale this 29th day of July 1675
in presence of us JOHN BAGWELL,   THOMAS T COOPER   Seale
        FRANCIS ʔ WEBB

Wee the Subscribers do depose and say that this within menconed Will was the last Will & Testament of THOMAS COOPER decd and that he was in pfect sence and memory at the signing & sealing thereof to the best of their Judgments As Witness our hands this 1st day of September 1675

JOHN BAGWELL
FRANCI ⟩ WEBB

Probatr p Sacramentium JOHN BAGWELL & FRANCIS WEBB in Cur Com Rappa primi die September 1675 et recordatr p me EDMUND CRASK Cl Cur

pp.   IN THE NAME OF GOD Amen I DENNIS SWELLIVANT of the County of Rappa &
183-   Parish of Farnham in Virga: Planter being weake in body but of perfect mind &
185   memory praised be God for it do here make my last Will & Testament in manner
         & form following
         Imprs. I bequeath my Soul to God my maker and my body to be buried in such
decent manner as my Executrix hereafter named shall think fitting and my worldly
goods as followeth
         Item I give & bequeath unto my Son DENNIS SWELLIVANT the land I now live on
from the lower pte thereof as farr as the place called by the name of DENNITS COVE with
the land I purchased of THOMAS FRESHWATER if when he come to the age of Sixteen
years he will accept thereof or else to have the upper part of my devident (Vizt) from
the sd DENNITS COVE to the upper end of my devident soe my sd Son DENNIS to have his
choice of either pts when the attain to the age of Sixteen years
         Item I give unto my Son DANIEL the upper pte of my Devident Vizt. from the sd
DENNITS COVE to the upper end provided my Son DENNIS doe not make choice thereof
and if he should then my sd Son DANIEL to have the other pte that I now live upon and
to Enjoy the same at the years of Sixteen but it is my will that neither of my sd Sons
shall dispose sell or convey away any parte thereof untill they attain to the age of one
& twenty years and if either of my sd Sonns should dye before they attaine to the sd age
of one & twenty years without issue then it is my will that the Survivour should enjoy
the whole
         Item I give & bequeath unto my Wife JOANE my whole personall estate during
the time she shall remain a widw. & if she shall happen to Marry then my personall
estate to be devided into three equall pts Vizt. my sd Wife one third and my sd Sons each
of them a third And if she shall die in time of her widdowhood then to be equally
devided between my two Sonns DENNIS & DANIEL.
         Item I give unto my Daughter SARAH the Wife of HENRY LENTON three Cowes &
one Steer of five or six years of age and I give unto my Grandson ANTHONY LENTON one
Cow
         Item I do make constitute & appoint my said Wife JOANE SWELLIVANT my sole
Executrix of this my last Will & Testament
         Item I doe hereby intrust my welbeloved Freinds Mr. ROBERT BAYLIE, Mr. JAMES
SAMFORD, HENRY LENTON & THOS. FRESHWATER as Overseers of this my Will and in con-
firmacon thereof have hereunto set my hand & Seale this first of December 1673
in presence of WILLIAM MAJOR,   DENNIS ⁊ SWELLIVANT   Seale
         JOHN HORYESLY

   I WILLIAM MAJOR do declare that I did see the within menconed DENNIS SWELLIVANT
sign Seal & publish the within menconed to be his last Will & Testament & that he was
in pfect mind & memory to the best of your deponents Judgment & further saith not
                              WILLIAM MAJOR
Probatr p Sacramentum WILLIAM MAJOR in Cur Com Rappa pmo die Septembr 1675 et
Recordatr p me EDMUND CRASKE Cl Cur Rappa

pp.   IN THE NAME OF GOD Amen I EDWARD JAMES being in perfect sence & memory do
185-   make & ordaine this my Last Will & Testament utterly denying all other Wills by
186   me made in manner & form as followeth
         Imprs first I bequeath my Soul to God that gave it me and my trust in Jesus
Christ my redeemer in hope of eternall Salvation
         I give and bequeath unto the Children of ROBERT WELCH, Sayler, living in Back
Street in BRISTOLL all my Estate both personall & reall onely I desire that ROBERT PECK

should have my estate in his possession till the abovesaid Children do come or send for
it and likewise I desire that ROBERT PECK as soone as he do hear of my decease that he
doe Imediately send the abovesd Children word of it & the sd ROBERT PECK do give a just
account to the Children of my sd Estate and to the confirmation hereof I have hereunto
sett my hand & seale this 1st day of March 1674/5
Signed sealed & delivered in
  presence of us JOHN PHILLIPS,   EDWARD JAMES   Seale
      ELIAS YATES

I ELIAS YATES do hereby declare that I did see the within menconed EDWARD JAMES
sign seal & publish the within mentioned as his last Will & Testament & that he was
then in perfect mind & memory to the best of my knowledge
                          ELIAS YATES
Probatr p Sacramentum ELIAS YATES 4 die November 1675

pp.   IN THE NAME OF GOD Amen I ROBERT PAYNE of the County of Rappa in Virginia
187-   Gent considerating the frailty of all flesh & the uncertain state of this transi-
191   tory life & knowing that I was born to die when it shall please God do make con-
        stitute ordain & declare this my last Will & Testamt. in manner & form following
revoaking and annulling by these presents all and every Testament and Testaments
Will and Wills heretofore by me made & declared either by word or writing & this is to
be taken only for my last Will & Testament & none other
    And first being penitent and sorry from the bottom of my heart for my Sins past
most humbly desiring forgiveness for the same I give and commit my Soule unto Almighty God my Saviour & redeemer in whom by the merritts of Jesus Christ I trust and
believe assuredly to be Saved & to have full remission & forgiveness of all my Sins and
that my Soule with my body at the generall day of resurrection shall rise again with joy
& through the merritts of Christs death & passion possess & inherit the Kingdom of
Heaven prpared for his elect & chosen
    my body I commit to the Earth to be buried in such place where it shall please
my Executrix hereafter named to appoint, and now for the setling of my temporall
Estate & such goods chattels and Debts as it hath pleased God farr above my deserts to
bestow upon me I do order give & dispose the same in manner & form following That is
to say
    first I will that all those debts & duties which I owe in right or conscience to any
manner of person or persons whatsoever shall be well and truely contented & paid or
ordained to be paid within convenient time after my decease by my Executris hereafter named
    Imprs. I give & bequeath unto my Son ROBERT PAYNE all and Singular my estate
as well lands as other my estate of what quality kind or condicon soever it be of within
this Colony of Virginia reserving to my Wife her accustomed third thereof onely
    Item my will is that both my land and other estate before & above bequeathed to
my Son ROBERT be enjoyed by him & his heirs for ever
    Item my will is that if my Son ROBERT depart this life before he attaine to one
and twenty years of age or have issue lawfully begotten that then I do give all and
Singular my sd lands & all and singular my other estate (excepting four thousand
pounds of tobacco & casque, which I will that my said Son ROBERT have delivered him at
the age of Sixteen years to improve his genius with by my Executrix hereafter named
out of my said Estate) unto my sd Loving Wife and her heirs for ever
    Item my will is that if my sd Son ROBERT shall depart this life before he attaine
to one and twenty years of age or before he hath issue lawfully begotten and that my sd

Wife allso shall die without more issue of her body lawfully begotten that then my will is that WILLIAM CLAPHAM, ALEXIA FLEMMING & MARY CLAPHAM enjoy all and singular my sd lands equally to be devided between them and to their heirs for ever

Item my will is that after my debts are paid that a division be made of my said personall estate and that what Servants especially and Catle belong to my said Son be put on some one of my best plantations and there managed for his interests & education & according to their cropps encreased in number of Servants and that the remainder of my other personall estate apptaining to my sd Son be disposed of by my said Executrix for the intrest of him & no otherwise and that my sd Son have Education allowed him Suitable to his Estate not impoverishing the same & that if he desire to enter thereon that he be suffered so to do when he shall by Gods grace attaine to the age of Seventeen years

Item my will is that if it shall please God that my Wife happen to be with Child during my life and that the same lives to full age or being a female to Sixteen years of age or day of marriage which shall happen first & have issue lawfully begotten that it have & enjoy fifteen hundred acres of land taking it together whereon I now live to it and its heirs for ever & one third pte of my psonall estate Excepting one Servant more to my sd Son ROBERT

Item I give the first mare foale that falls of my Sorrell mare to MARY MEEDOR my God Daughter with all its increase to her & her heirs for ever

Item I give the second mare foale that comes of my sd Mare to MARY CLAPHAM & her increase for ever & her heirs for ever

Item I give the fourth Mare foale that shall come of my sd Mare to ELIZABETH MADESTARD with her increase to her & her heirs for ever

Item I do hereby nominate appoint and ordain my well beloved Wife ELIZABETH PAYNE Sole Executrix of this my Last Will & Testament desiring Mr. WARWICK CAMOCK to see that this my Will be performed in all respects as neare & as fully as can be & that whatsoever person shall intermarry with my Wife be compelled to give Bond with good Securitie for performance hereof he be invested with any part of my Son ROBERTs estate & that if Mr. CAMOCK die before that the Court of Rappa. see the same effected which is also my will so to be done

Item my will is that my Son ROBERT have from the time of my departure of this life as well the male as female increase of his mare Rose & to him & his heirs for ever

In Witness of all & singular the prmises I the sd ROBERT PAYNE have hereunto put my hand & Seale this 24th day of March 1671
Signed sealed & publish:ed
in presence of us RICHARD BARBER   ROBERT PAYNE   Seale
         JOHN MEADOR

JOHN MEADOR aged 38 years & RICHARD BARBER aged 30 yeares or thereabouts depose & say that this within written is the last Will & Testament of Mr. ROBERT PAYNE formerly Clerk of this County and that he was in prfect sence and memory to the best of their knowledge when he signed sealed & published the same

                         JOHN MEADOR
                         RICHARD BARBER
Probatr p Sacramentum JOHN MEADOR & RICHARD BARBER 4 die Novembr 1675
et Recordatr   Test EDMD CRASKE Cl Cur

pp.   IN THE NAME OF GOD Amen I HENRY COX being very sick and weake in body but
191-   of good and perfect memory thanks be given to Almighty God therefore I do
194   make and ordain this my last Will and Testament in manner & form following

first I commit my Soule into the hands of Almighty God who made me & who through the alone merritts of Christ I trust will also save me and my body to be decently buried at the discretion of my Executors hereafter mentioned And as touching those worldly goods which God in his mercy hath lent me I freely & willingly dispose of them as followeth

First I will & my meaning is that whereas EDMUND CRASK Clerk of Rappa County standeth engaged with me that I shall make a good assurance of the one half or moyetie of my land I now live upon unto Mr. JOHN HASSLEWOOD for & in consideracon of his deliverering up of a Certain Bond of mine of Five hundred pounds Sterling bearing date the 8th of July 1673 as allso for the passing of Bills of Exchange for the payment of Forty Five pounds Sterling mony to me or my Order now my will is that my Executors hereafter named make good the sale of the moyetie or halfe part of my land according to obligation and save the sd EDMUND CRASK harmless and indemnifyed from the sd Mr. JOHN HASLEWOOD his heirs or assignes or otherwise take care for the Satisfaction of the sd HASLEWOOD his just Debt & take in the Bond as aforesd & for non performance thereof then I will & my meaning is that the sd EDMUND CRASK shall be possessed with so much of my Estate both reall & personall as shall discharge & satisfie the obligacon wherein he stands engaged with me to the sd HASLEWOOD untill such time as the sd Debt be satisfied & the sd CRASK saved harmless from all such charges or damages he shall be at by being become bound with me as aforesaid

Item I give unto Mr. JAMES MILLER now living with me my Sword & belt to be delivered him immediately after my death

Item I give unto my Brother in Law RICHARD CAWTHORN my best Cloath suite my best hatt & a pair of French falls, & a pair of Stockins both new to be delivered him immedately after my death

Item I give unto RICHARD CAWTHORN JUNR. my Nephew and to AURELIA CAWTHORN my neece each of them a Cow Calfe to be delivered them about the begining of June next after my death

Item I give & bequeath unto Mr. THOMAS GORDON of Rappa. County & to Mrs. JANE GORDON his Wife each of them Tenn shillings to buy them two mourning rings to be paid them by my Executors within two months after my decease

Item I give unto my friend EDMUND CRASK twenty shillings to buy him a Mourning ring to be paid him by my Executors within two months after my decease

Item all the rest of my Estate both reall & personall as lands goods Chattels Catle & all impliments of household stuff or husbandry bills bonds ready mony & debts oweing me I freely and willing give & bequeath them all to my Executors hereafter named for and during their naturall lives & after their decease to WILLIAM COX my Son hereby willing & requiring my sd Son WILLIAM within one year after he shall be possessed of my Estate as aforesd to give unto the Child my Wife now goeth with a good assurance of the moietie of the land he shall be possessed withall by this my Will or the value thereof (as two men indifferently chosen shall adjudge it worth) at the discretion of my sd Son but if the sd Child should happen to die before my sd Son WILLIAM shall be possessed with my Estate as aforesaid then the whole Estate to be & remaine unto my Son WILLIAM & his heirs forever

Lastly I do hereby make & appoint my Father in Law WILLIAM STRACHEY of GLOCESTER COUNTY and ARABELLA COX my now Wife joynt Executors of this my last Will & Testament hereby willing and requiring them to pay all such debts as I shall justly happen to owe at the time of my death to take care of and provide for my Children during their minorities & to bring my body decently to the ground and it is my earnest desire that my Father in Law would come and live with my wife & assist her in the management of her estate

And this revoaking all other Will or Wills heretofore by me made either by word of mouth or writing I declare this to be my last Will & Testament

In Witness whereof I have hereunto sett my hand & affixed my Seal this two and twentieth day of February 1674

Signes sealed & published   HENRY COX   Seale
in presence of us CORNELIUS MELAGHLEN
    WILLIAM HARDING, THOMAS HART

I WILL HARDING aged 28 years or thereabout and I THOMAS HART aged 25 years or thereabout do depose and say that we did see the within mentioned HENRY COX sign seal & publish the within mentioned to be his last Will & Testament & that he was in perfect sence & memory at the signing sealing & publishing thereof to the best of our Judgments As Witness our hands this 2d of November 1675

                                                        WM. HARDING
                                                        THOMAS HART

Probatr. p Sacrament GULIEB HARDING et THOMS HART 2 die Novembr 1675 et recordatr 4 die Xbris

pp.   IN THE NAME OF GOD Amen I THOMAS PAGE being very sick in body but of per-
195-   fect memory glory be to God do make & ordaine this my last Will and Testament
196   Imprs. I do give unto RICHD. WEST Eldest Daughter of ELIZABETH WEST one Cow
    with her increase being called Starr
        Item I do give unto CORNELIUS NOELLs Eldest Daughter MARY NOELL one Cow
    with her increase being called Violett
        Item I god give unto my Grandchild SAMUELL ALLEN my Plantation & land be-
    longing to it wch I formerly lived upon to him and his heirs forever.
        Item I do give unto my Son VALENTINE ALLEN two hundred acres of land where
    he now live to him & his heirs for ever
        Item I do give unto WILLIAM HODGEs Children three hundred acres of land
    being part of a Devident where my Sonn ALLEN now live to be equally divided between
    them I doe give it to them & their heirs for ever
        Item all the rest of my estate my debts being paid I doe give unto my Daughter
    MARY ALLEN & her heirs for ever
        Item I doe make my Daughter MARY ALLEN my sole Executrix
As Witness my hand & seale this 10th day of March 1676
Witness WILLIAM FOGGE   THOMAS PAGE   Seale
    ROBERT R REDERFORD

    Wee the Subscribers do depose and say that wee did see the above menconed Testator seale sign & publish the abovesaid Will to be his last Will & Testament & that he was in perfect sence & memory at the signing sealing and publishing thereof to the best of our Judgments

                                                    WILLIAM FOGGE
                                                    ROBERT R RUDDERFORD

Jurantr in Cur Com Rappa 3 die 1676 Recordatr xx die May 1676
A probate hereon is granted to Capt. THOMAS HAWKINS upon MARY ALLENs consent

pp.   IN THE NAME OF GOD Amen I JOHN BERRIDGE being Sick & weak of body doth
196-   make this my last Will & Testament in manner & form following
197   Imprs. I bequeath my Soule to Almighty God my Creator wherein & through
    the merrits of Christ Jesus my Saviour I hope to inherit eternall life

Item I bequeath my body to my mother Earth to be decently interred & buried as for my worldly goods I give in manner and form following

Item I give unto my loveing friend FRANCIS SUTTLE all that debt of tobacco that is due to me from HENRY DURRANT

Item I give unto my loveing friend JANE BARRETT all that she hath in her possession of mine

Item I give & bequeath unto my loveing Friend RICHARD MATHEWS two Bills one of WILLIAM TALBUTT that 1100 lb of tobo, & one of ROBERT MOSS that 1200 lb tobacco & one gun at ROBERT MOSSes

It. All the rest of my Estate I give & bequeath to my loveing friend FRANCIS SUTTLE making & ordaining of him my full and sole Executor

In Witness whereof I have set my hand & Seale this 20th of March 1675/6

Signed sealed & deld

in presence of us   JOHN BERRIDG   Seale
    JOHN STONE
        WALTER TURNER

Wee underwritten do depose and say that wee did see the within named Testator sign seal & publish the within mentioned to be his last Will & Testament & that he was in perfect sence & memory at the signing sealing & publishing thereof to the best of our Judgments

                                            JOHN STONE
                                            WALTER TURNER

Jurantr JOH STONE et WALT TURNER in Cu com Rappa 2 did Maii Ano: 1676
Probatr & recordatr xx die

pp.   IN THE NAME OF GOD Amen I JOHN SHERLOCK of the County of Rappa & Parish of
198-   FARNHAM being very sick & weak but in true and parfect memory praised be
199   God for it and knowing the frailty of this life do here make my last Will & Testament in manner and form as followeth

Imprimis I give & bequeath my Soule to the Almighty God my maker in hopes of resurrection in and through my Lord & Saviour Jesus Christ my worldly goods I dispose of as followeth

I give and bequeath to my son ANDREW SHERLOCK three hundred & Sixty (years) of land & do appoint my Wife shall have her being & lively hood upon the said land during her life without molestacon and after hir decease do order ANDREW SHURLOCK to be full & wholy executor & administr thereof

I give and bequeath to my Sonn JOHN SHURLOCK fifty acres of land joying upon WILLIAM DAVIS land to him & his heirs for ever

I give and bequeath all my Catle & hoggs to my Wife & my Son ANDREW SHERLOCK & do appoint that they shall be equally devided when ANDREW is of age

I give & bequeath to my Son JOHN's Children, HANNA & JOHN, One Cow Calfe belonging to Cherry & this Calfe to run till the girl is married or mariagable & to be equally devided between the boy & the girle my Son JOHN having the male increase for looking after them

I give and bequeath to my Son BARTHOLOMEW LEALURs Children, JOHN and BARTHOLOMEW, one cow calfe and do appoint that the female increase shall be equally devided between them when they are of age & their Father to have the male for looking after them

I give and bequeath one Cow & Calfe that is to JOHN JONES towards building a house for my Wife & ANDREW to live in & all my moveables to be equally devided be-

tween my Son ANDREW & my Wife and for my Debts I leave Bills to pay them with my
Wife of THOMAS FRESHWATER & HEZEKIAH TURNER and this I do declare to be my last
Will & Testamt. As Witness my hand this 7th of January 1675
prsence of EDWARD JONES,   JOHN ┼ SHURLOCK   Seale
        WILLIAM X X BRAY

I EDWARD JONES do testifie that I did see the within mentioned JOHN SHURLOCK SENR.
signe seale & publish this his last Will & Testament & that he was then in perfect mind
& memory to the best of this deponents Judgment
                                                        EDWARD JONES
    Juratis est JONES in Cu Com Rappa 3 die May 1676
    Probabr et recordatr xx die

pp.   IN THE NAME OF GOD Amen I THOMAS ERWIN of the Parish of Sittingburn in the
200-   County of Rappa being sick in body but of sound & perfect memory do hereby
202   make & ordain this my last Will & Testament hereby revoaking and making void
        any Testament heretofore by me made either by word or writing & this onely to
be taken for my Last Will and Testament (my Wife to be my only Executrix hereafter).
        Imprs. I give and bequeath my Soule into the hands of Almighty God hoping
and trusting through the mercies of Jesus Christ to obtaine full and perfect remission
of all my Sinns & my Body to the earth from whence it was taken to be buried in comely
and decent manner according to the discretion of my Wife & Relations And as for my
worldly goods I thus bequeath them
        Item I give and bequeath to my Wife one bay mare & if in case she bring forth a
mare foale it to run for the good of all my Children and likewise there be three mares
more & a horse which I do order & constitute to be given to my Children in generall & a
young gelding in the same manner for the use of my Children
        Item I give & bequeath to my Children eight Cows & their increase & them to be
kept upon my said Plantation for the use of all my Children & no exception to be made
but equally to be devided
        Item I give & bequeath to my two Eldest Sonns all my land consisting of Two
hundred & thirty acres & the said land to be equally devided when they come of age that
is to say Sixteen yeares & then to be free to enjoy accordingly to live together upon one
Plantation, that then my Eldest Sonn provide proportionably so much land in some
other place convenient as my Second Sonn thinks fitt otherwise to concurr to live
unanimously together according to will & desire
        Item it is my will & command that my Wife have the third part of the land & half
the Orchard for the use of her and likewise her children for ever without any molestation whatsoever
        Item I give & bequeath to my two youngest Sonns two hundred acres of land
lying in the READY WAY to Collo. WASHINGTONs & if it please God they should depart
before they come of age to enjoy it then the said land to fall to my two Eldest Sons and if
in case they should die then it to go to the use of my Daughters
        Item it is my will that my Wife shall have all my personall estate that is to say
all cattle hoggs & all moveables whatsoever as tobaccoes debts dues & whatsoever be-
longs to me in order to the education & bringing up of the Children
        Item I doe hereby make ordain & appoint my loveing Wife ANN ERWIN the
whole Executrix of this my last Will and Testament to see it performed & further I do
ordaine appoint my loveing Freind JOHN MATLIN & WILLIAM SERJEANT & HENRY
CREIGHTON Overseers & Assistants to my Wife & in case of the death of my Wife to take
care of my Childrens Estate & Education

In Witness whereof I have hereunto set my hand & Seale this 19th of January
1675
Signed sealed & delivered to be   THOMAS ✗ ERWIN   Seale
  his last Will & Testament
in presence of us JOHN PAYNE
          THOMAS BARKER

I Underwritten do depose and say that I did see the within named Testatr. signe seale &
publish the within mentioned to be his last Will & Testament & that he was in prfect
sence & memory at the signing sealing & publishing thereof to the best of my
Judgment

                              JOHN PAYNE

 Juratr est PAYNE in Cur Com Rappa 3 die May 1676
Probatr et recordatr xx die

pp.   IN THE NAME OF GOD Amen this 26th of June 1675 I JOHN HULL being well in
202-   body and of good and perfect memory thanks be to Almighty God & calling to
205   remembrance the uncertainty of this transitory life & that all flesh must yeild
       unto death when it shall please God to call do make constitute and declare this
my last Will & Testament in manner & form following & first being penitent and Sorry
from the bottom of my heart for my Sinns past most humbly desireing forgiveness for
the saime I give and commit my Soule to Almighty God my Saviour and redeemer in
whom & by the merritts of Jesus Christ I trust and believe assuredly to be saved, & to
have full remission & forgiveness of all my Sinns and that my Soule with my body at
the general day of resurrection shall rise again with joy & through the merritts of
Christ death and passion possess & inherit the Kingdom of Heaven prepared for his
elect & chosen and my body to be buried where it shall please my Executrix hereafter
named to appoint and now for the setling of my temporall Estate & such lands goods
chattels & debts as it hath pleased God farr above my deserts to bestow upon me I do
order and give and dispose the same in manner and forme following that is to say
       first I will that all those debts due to any manner of person or persons shall be
well contented & paid by my Executrix hereafter named
       Item My Will and desire is my Son in Law JOHN CARTER be paid his five hundred
pounds due to him for his Wives Dower according to Specialty but if it should so fall out
that what inquests & debts & returnable goods will not pay it without disposeing of my
Wifes plate and Jewills then my will is that part of the land be sold to pay it
       Item I give unto my Son JOHN CARTER & his Wife each of them a Ring of forty
shillings price
       Item I give unto my loveing Wife ELIZABETH HULL all the plate & Jewills I die
possessedof
       Item I give & bequeath to my Son ROGER HULL & his heirs forever all my land I
die possessed of
       Item I give & bequeath unto my loveing Wife ELIZABETH HULL & my Son ROGER
HULL all my monies goods & chattels I die possessed of my debts & legacies being first
paid equally to be devided between them
       Item my will is that my Loveing Wife ELIZABETH HULL may have any of my
Plantations with the land & houses belonging to the same that she will make choice of
during her life & then returne to my Son ROGER HULL or his heirs
       And I do appoint my loveing Wife ELIZABETH HULL Executrix of this my Last Will
as Witness my hand & Seale the day & year above written

Signed sealed & acknowledged
  in presence of us THOMAS COLLINS   JOHN HULL   seale
            THO: SMITH

The Within named THOMAS COLLINS aged 22 years & THO: SMITH aged 22 years or
thereabouts sworn & examined that they did see the within named Lt. Coll. JOHN HULL
sign seale & publish the within mentioned as his last Will and Testament & that he was
in perfect sence & memory at the signing & sealing thereof to the best of your Deponts.
Judgments and further saith not

                                          THOS. COLLINS
                                          THO: SMITH

Jurati THO: COLLINS et THO: SMITH in Cu Com Rappa 3 die Maii 1677
Probatr p Scratment THO: COLLINS & THO: SMITH et recordatr x8 die Junii

pp.   IN THE NAME OF GOD Amen the 22d day of January 1672/3 I RICHARD SIMMS
205-   being sick in body but of sound & perfect memory praise be given to God for the
206   same and knowing the uncertainty of this life on earth & being desirous to
         settle things in order to make this my last Will & Testament in manner & form
following that is to say
         First and Principally I commend my Soul to Almighty God my Creator assuredly
beleiving that I shall receive full pardon and free remission of my Sins and be saved by
the pretious death & merritts of my Blessed Saviour and redeemer Christ Jesus and my
body to the Earth from whence it was taken to be buried in such decent Christian manner as to my Exers hereafter named shall be thought meet and convenient. And as
touching such worldly Estate as the Lord in Mercy hath lent me my will & meaning is
the same shall be employed and bestowed as hereafter by this my Will is expressed and
first I do revoake renounce frustrate & make void all Wills be me formerly made and declare and appoint this my last Will & Testament
         Imprs. I will that all those debts that I owe in right to any manner of person or
persons be well and truely contented & paid within convenient time after my decease
by my Executor hereafter named
         I give & bequeath unto JOHN PENN if it shall please God I dye without wife or
issue all my reall and personall estate that is to say lands goods & Chattels as well
moveable as unmoveable which is properly mine to his heirs & assignes for ever And
do heereby ordain my well beloved Freind JOHN PEN to be my sole Executor of this my
Will & Testament & none other as Witness my hand & Seale the day abovesaid
Signed & sealed in the
  presence of us THO: HARWARE   RICHARD RS: SIMMS   Seale
           HENRY WILLIAMSON

The within named THOMAS HARWARE aged 34 yeares or thereabouts & HENRY WIL-
LIAMSON aged 34 or thereabouts sworn & examined saith that they did see the within
mentioned RICHARD SIMMS sign seale & publish the within named Will as his last Will
& Testament and that he was in perfect sence & memory at the signing & sealing
thereof to the best of their Judgmts. & further saith not

                                          THO: HARWARE
                                          HENRY WILLIAMSON

Jurati HENRI WILLIAMSON et THOMAS HARWARE 3 di Maii 1677
Recordatr xx die Junii

pp. IN THE NAME OF GOD Amen JOHN PEN in the County of Rappa. being sick & weake
206- in body but in perfect memory praised be to God for it do make this my last Will
208 and Testament first I bequeath my Soule to Almighty God that gave it me in
hopes of a Joyfull resurrection through the merrits of Jesus Christ my redeemer
my body to the ground from whence it was taken As for my temporall Estate which hath
pleased God to bestow upon mee I give & bequeath as following

first I give and bequeath unto ANNE SHARP Daughter of JOHN SHARP my Plantation which I now live on & fifty pounds Sterling money of England.

I give and bequeath unto JUDITH SHARP the Daughter of JOHN SHARP decd fifty
pounds Sterling money of England.

I give & bequath unto ELIZABETH HARWARE the Daughter of THOMAS HARWARE
fifty pounds Sterling money of England the abovesd three fifty pounds & the plantation
to be delivered at the day of their marriages by my Executor hereafter named

I give and bequeath unto EDWARD DRACAS One Cow to be delivered upon demand

I give & bequeath unto THOMAS COCKER one Cow to be delivered upon demand

I give & bequeath unto MARY PEYTON one Cow to be delivered upon demand and
likewise she the said MARY to be free at my decease for all other my movables Stock
Catle & hogs horses & mares & Servants & what else either in Virginia, MARILAND,
England or elsewhere I give & bequeath unto my beloved Friend THOMAS HARWARE
& his heirs for ever onely he paying my debts which I owe in right to any man And do
hereby constitute nominate & ordain my said Freind THOS. HARWARE to be whole & sole
Exre. of this my last Will & Testament making void all other & this to be my last Will &
no other further I give unto THO: TALBUTT the Son of WILLIAM TALBUTT a young Mare
about three years old and likewise two Cows to be delivered upon demand and for my
land which I have given to ANNE SHARP if it should please God to die without issue I
give to my Freind THOMAS HARWARE otherwise to shee & her heirs forever. As witness
my hand & Seale this 13th day of January 1676/7

Test PETER HOPEGOOD.   JOHN PENN   Seale
      JOSEPH PRICE

  The Within named PETER HOPEGOOD aged 30 years or thereabout & JOSEPH PRICE aged
26 yrs. or thereabts. sworn & examined saith that they did see the within named JOHN
PENN sign seal & publish the within mentioned to be his last Will & Testament & that he
was in perfect sence & memory at the signing & sealing thereof to the best of your
deponts. Judgments & further saith not
                                        PETER HOPGOOD
                                        JOSEPH PRICE
  Jurati PET HOPGOOD & JOSEPH PRICE in Cu Com Rappa 29 die Maii 1677
Recordatr xx die Junii 1677

pp. IN THE NAME OF GOD Amen I ROBERT BISHOP of the County of Rappa in the Parish
209- of Farnham being Sicke & weake in body but of perfect disposeing memory do
210 make this my last Will & Testament in manner following

  Imprs. I bequeath my Soule to God by the hope I have in Jesus Christ my
Saviour & redeemer hoping for pardon of all my Sins & my body to the Earth to be
buried with Christian buriall and for the estate it hath please God the Almighty to
bestow upon me after my just debts & funerall charges paid & Satisfyed I give & bequeath in manner & form following

  Item I give my land that I bought of Mr. HENRY AWBERY unto JOHN GRIGORY
JUNIOR unto him & his heirs for ever and likewise all my personall Estate and he to be
my lawfull Executor & this will to cutt of all other Wills & Testaments whatsoever

wherein to I have sett my hand & seale this 21st of Aprill in the year of or. Lord God
1676
Signed, sealed & delivered
  in presence of THO: WHEELER   ROBERT S BISHOP   Seale
      JOHN GARNER,. JOHN BURNITT

The deposition of THOMAS WHEELER aged 30 years or thereabouts, JOHN GARNER aged
25 yeares or thereabouts Sworn & examined Saith that they did see the within mentioned ROBERT BISHOP sign, seale and publish the within mentioned to be his last Will &
Testament & that he was in perfect sence and memory as the signing sealing & publishing thereof to the best of their Judgments
                              THO: WHEELER
                              JOHN GARNER

  Jurati in Cu Com Rappa 6 die Junii 1677 et Probatr
recordatr xx die

pp.   KNOW ALL MEN by these presents that I ROBERT BISHOP of the County of Rappa
210- do upon my death bed make JOHN GRIGORY JUNR. my lawfull Executor & do give
211   him power & Command to demand & receive 285 pound of good tobo. of JOHN
        JONES my Brother in Law which is to be paid by the 10th of October 1676 & the
sd JOHN GRIGORY is to produce an heifer with the sd tobo. for the use of JOHN JONES
JUNR. with the increase of the said Heifer untill the sd JOHN shall come of age and likewise I ROBERT BISHOP give JOHN GRIGORY JUNR. order to receive one Heifer which is at
Capt. JOHN GRIGORYs Pen marked with a Cropp & a Slitt on the left eare one yeare old of
a red Colour with her increase male and female when the sd JOHN JONES shall come of
age and likewise one Sow when the sd JOHN JONES shall come of age & the sd JOHN
GRIGORY to keep the sd 2 Heifers with their increase untill the sd JOHN JONES shall
come of age then to deliver them unto him with their increase. As Witness my hand &
seale this 24th of May 1676
Sealed, Signed & delivered   ROBT. S BISHOP   Seale
  in presence of THO: WHEELER
       RICHD. GRIGORY
Recordatr xx die Junii Ano 1677

pp.   IN THE NAME OF GOD Amen This being the Last Will and Testament of PETER
211- MILLS being very sick in body & weak but of perfect memory.
213   Imprs. I bequeath my body to the Earth & my Spirit to God that gave it
      Item I give & bequeath all my whole Estate both personall & reall unto my
Sister ELIZABETH MILLS onely I give & bequeath unto MARY BORKETT the Daughter of
my Bro: JOHN BORKETT the youngest Mare filly that now is & likewise one black yearling heifer to JANE WALL the Wife of SAMUEL WALL.
      I give and bequeath unto MARY RAW the Calfe that come of the Cow cald Stoaze
being a Cow Calfe likewise I give and bequeath unto RICHARD MIDDLETON one Sow
Shoate
      I give and bequeath unto my Brother BURKETT my old Sow & to my Father two
young barrows & to JOHN MILLS one young red Sow and to JOSEPH SHIPP a young Sow
likewise I give and bequeath unto SAMUEL WARD two yearlings which my Sister
MARGARET gave to me likewise I doe desire that my Sister ELIZABETH MILLS may have
possession of all my Estate soe soone as I am ded & to live where she pleases likewise I do
desire that my Executrix ELIZABETH MILLS will pay the Doctor and other necessary
Charges for my funerall

Signed, sealed & delivered   PETER P MILLS   Seale
 in the presence of us February 2, 1676
Test SAM WARD
     JOHN MILLS

       I the within mentioned SAM WARD do hereby declare that I did see the within named
PETER MILLS sign Seale & publish this within Specifyed as his last Will & Testament And
that he was then in perfect mind & memory to the best of this deponents Judgment
                                              SAM WARD

       I the Subscriber do delcare that I did see the within mentioned PETER MILLS publish
the within written as his last Will & Testament & that was then in perfect mind &
memory to the best of this deponents Judgment
                                              JOHN MILLS
     Jurati SAM WARD et JOHAN MILLS in Cu Com Rappa 2 die May 1677
et recordatr xxi die Junii

pp.   IN THE NAME OF GOD Amen I NATHANIEL BAXTER of the Parish of Farnham in the
213-   County of Rappa Planter being by Gods grace intended forth for the Warrs do
216   make and ordain this my last Will & Testament in manner & form following
       Imprs. I bequeath my Soule unto Almighty God who gave it in full & certaine
hopes in and through the merritts of Jesus to inheritt Eternall life and my body to return to the Earth and likewise it is my will & I do hereby give & bequeath unto my
naturall Sonn NATHANIEL BAXTER & his heirs for ever all the bounds of my land from
PISCATAWAY CREEK unto Mr. PARRYS LITTLE CREEK and the remainder of my Devident
of land which lyeth on the other side of Mr. PARRYS CREEK towards THOMAS DAYES
formerly HUTTSONs by Virtue hereof I will & bequeath unto my Daughter ANN BAXTER
& to the heirs of her body lawfully begotten for ever Provided Allways & my desire is
that if it shall please God to take to his Mercy either my Son NATHANIELL or my Daughter ANNE before they be of age of one and twenty years or be married the first of them
so dyeing his or her part of the land abovesd shall fall & descend to the Survivor for
ever
       Likewise it is my will & I do bequeath unto my well beloved Wife one gray stone
horse with a small slitt in the right eare & a black pied heifer comonly called by the
name of Tilt with all her increase to be wholly at her own disposeing
       Item I do give & bequeath unto my Daughter ELETHIAS BAXTER one Cow
comonly known by the name of Cherry with all her increase male & female to her &
her heirs for ever in case the sd Cow shall die without any increase then the sd
ELETHIAS to have a Heifer out of the Stock with her increase male and female for ever
Provided allwayes & it is my desire that in case the sd ELETHIAS shall die without issue
then the sd Cow or Heifer to return with their increase to my abovesd Children
       I doe further by this last Will & Testament give and bequeath unto my Wife in
the leiw of her thirds & to my above named Sonn & Daughter NATHANIEL & ANNE
equally to be devided after my debts satisfyed all my pesonall estate moovable and im-
moovable for ever
       And I do further appoint my dear and well beloved Wife with NATHANIEL & ANN
my Son & Daughter Executors of this my last Will and Testament and likewise my well
beloved Freinds Mr. WILLIAM YOUNG SENR. & THOMAS ROBERTS to see this my Will
executed
       In Witness whereof I have hereunto sett my hand & Seale this 22 of May Ano
Dom 1676

Signed, sealed & delivd.   NATHANIELL BAXTER   Seale
  in presence of THO. *ThJENKINS*
   JOHN JOLLY, BARBARY ∞ ANDREWS

THOMAS ROBERTS aged 28 years or thereabout being sworn & examined saith that your
Depont. did write & see the within mentioned NATHANIEL BAXTER signe seale & publish
the same as his last Will & Testament in the presence of THOMAS JENKINS, JOHN JOLLY &
BARBARY ANDREWS who in his prsence did witness the same & further yr. Depont.
saith not

                 THO: ROBERTS

  Juratus est THO: ROBERTS in Cur Com Rappa 2 die May 1677
Probatr p Sacrament pr THOM ROBERTS et recordatr xx die Junii

pp.   IN THE NAME OF GOD AMEN I GEORGE JACKSON being Sick in body but in perfect
216-   sence & memory do acknoweldge this to be my last Will and Testament I do com-
217   mitt my Soule unto God my flesh and body unto the earth & wormes
    I doe make EDWARD FREEMAN my whole & sole Executor & likewise I do be-
queath & give unto ROBT. EAID Sonne in Law to the sd EDWARD FREEMAN one hundred
acres of land betwixt the sd ROBERT EAID & EDWARD FREEMAN Lawfull Son the sd ED-
WARD FREEMAN
Test THO: X HARPER,   GEORGE ⅂ JACKSON
   SYMON ⅊ BUTLER

  The Within named THOMAS HARPER aged 50 yeares or thereabouts being sworn & examined saith that he did see the within named GEORGE JACKSON sign seale & publish the
within mentioned to be his last Will & Testament yt. he was in perfect sence & memory
at the Signing & Sealing thereof to the best of his Judgmt: & further saith not
             THO: X HARPER

  Juratis est HARPER in Cur Com Rappa 2 die Maii 1677
Probatr & Sacrament THO HARPER 3 et recordatr xxi die Junii 1677

pp.   THE DEPOSITION of ELETHIA PERKINS aged 49 years or thereabouts that your
217-   Depont. being in the house when THOMAS JENKINS did make his Will in Writing
218   & did heare him give his whole Estate to his Sonn in Law WM. PRICE after the
    decease of his Mother or day of Marriage onely two Cows & a Calfe to WILLIAM
PRICE his Sisters Children & further your depont. saith not
           ELETHIA Ŧ PERKINS
  Juratus ELETHIAS PERKINS in Cur Com Rappa 2 die May 1677
et Recodatr xxi die Junii

  THE DEPOSITION of THOMAS ROBERTS aged 28 or thereabouts Sworn & Examined saith
that yor depont. did write & witness a Will of THO: JENKINS wherein he did give all his
Estate to his Son in Law WM. PRICE after the death of his Wife onely excepted two Cows
or heifers which were given to WM. PRICE his Sisters Children & further yre Depont.
saith not
            THO: ROBERTS
  Juratus est THO: ROBERTS in Cu Com Rappa 2 die May 1677
et recordatr xxi die Junii

pp. The Three and twentieth day of February. IN THE NAME OF GOD Amen I THOMAS
218- ELLWERD lying very sick & weak do comit my body to the ground & my Soule to
219 the Almighty and this is my Will and Testimony to give unto my Daughter BETTY
     one hundred ackres of my land begining at the further side of the devidend of
the sd land and one brown heifer of three years old & her increase & all the rest that I
have besides to be devided between my Wife & my Son & my Wife to have the disposing
of it till my Son comes to age. Given undr. my hand this 23 day of February Ano Dm
1675
Test THOMAS NAYLOR,   THOMAS I ELLVERD
     SUSANNA WHITE

  The abovenamed THOMAS NAYLOR aged thirty five years or thereabouts & SUSANNA
WHITE 29 years or thereabout being sworn & examined saith that they did see the above
named THOMAS ELLWERD sign & publish the above mentioned as his Last Will & Testament & that he was in perfect Sence & memory at the signing thereof to the best of
your Deponts. Judgment & further saith not
                                          THO: NAYLOR
                                          SUSANNA WHITE
  Jurati THO: NAYLOR & SUSANNA WHITE in Cu Com Rappa 2 die Maii 1677
et recordatr xxi die Junii

pp. IN THE NAME OF GOD AMEN I LAWRENCE WASHINGTON of the County of Rappa.
219- being Sick & weak of body but of sound & perfect memory do make & ordain this
224 my last Will & Testament hereby revoaking annulling & making void all former
     Wills and Coddicells heretofore by me made either by Word or writing & this
only to be taken for my last Will and Testament
     Imprs. I give and bequeath my Soule into the hands of Almighty God hoping
and trusting through the mercy of Jesus Christ my one Savior. and Redeemer to receive
full pardon & forgiveness of all my Sinns and my body to the earth to be buried in
comely & decent manner by my Executrix hereafter named & for my worldly goods I
thus dispose them
     Item I give and bequeath unto my loving Daughter MARY WASHINGTON my
whole Estate in England both reall & personall to her & the heirs of her body lawfully
begotten for ever to be delivered to her possession imediately after my decease by my
Executrix hereafter named
     I give and bequeath unto my aforesd Daughter MARY WASHINGTON my Smallest
Stone ring & one Silver Cup now in my possession to her & her hairs for ever to be delivered to her imediately after my decease
     I give and bequeath unto my loveing Son JOHN WASHINGTON all my bookes to
him & his heirs forever to be delivered to him when he shall come to the age of Twenty
one yeares
     I give and bequeath unto my Son JOHN & Daughter ANN WASHINGTON all the rest
of my Plate but what is before exprest to be equally devided between them & delivered
into their possession when they come of age
     Item my will is that all my debts which of right & justice I owe to any man be
justly & truely paid as allso my funerall expences after which my will is that all my
whole Estate both reall and personall be equally devided between my loveing Wife JANE
WASHINGTON & the two Children God hath given me by her Vizt. JOHN & ANN WASHING-
TON
     I give & bequeath it all to them & the heires of their bodies lawfully begotten
for ever, my Sonns part to be delivered when he comes of age, & my Daughters when

she come of age or day of mariage which shall first happen

Item my will is that that land which became due to me in right of my Wife lying on the South side of the River formerly belonging to Capt. LAWRENCE FLEMMING & commonly known by the name of WEST FALIO be sold by my Executrix hereafter named for the payment of my debts imediately after my decease

Item my will is that the land I have formerly entred with Capt. WM. MOSELY be forthwith after my decease surveyed & Pattented by my Execr. hereafter named & if it shall amount to the quanity of one thousand acres then I give & bequeath unto ALEXANDER BARROW two hundred acres of the land to him & his heirs for ever the remainder I give & bequeath unto my loveing Wife and my two Children to them & their heirs for ever to be equally devided between them

Item my will is that if it shall please God to take my Daughter MARY out of this world before she comes of age with no heirs of hir body lawfully begotten then I give & bequeath my land in England which by my Will I have given to her unto my Sonne JOHN WASHINGTON & his heirs & the psonall efects which I have given to hir I give & bequeath the same unto my Daughter ANN WASHINGTON & her heirs forever.

Item I do hereby make & ordain my Loveing Wife JANE WASHINGTON Executrix of this my last Will & Testament to see it performed and I doe hereby make & appoint my dear and loveing Brother Coll. JOHN WASHINGTON & my loveing Freind THOMAS HAW-KINS (in case of the death or neglect of my Executrix) to be the Overseers and Guardians of my Children untill they come of age to the truth whereof I have hereunto sett my hand & Seale this 27th of September 1675

　　　　　　　　　　　　　　　　LAWRENCE WASHINGTON　　　Seale

Signed Sealed & declared to be his
 last Will & Testament in the presence of us
　　　CORNELIUS WOOD,
　　　JOHN BARROW,　　　　　　　A CODICIL of the Last Will & Testament of
　　　HENRY TANDY JUNR.　　　　　LAURENCE WASHINGTON annext to his Will
　　　　　　　　　　　　　　　　　made September 27th 1675

Item my will is that my part of the land I now live uipon which became due to me by marriage of my Wife I leave it wholy & solely to her disposall after my decease. As Witness my hand the day & year above written
Signed sealed & Declared to be a Codicil
 of my Last Will & Testament　　　　　LAWRENCE WASHINGTON　　　Seale
in the presence of us CORNELIUS WOOD,
　　　HENRY TANDY JUNR.

The abovenamed HENRY TANDY JUNR. aged 17 years or thereabts. Sworn & examined saith that he did see the abovenamed LAURENCE WASHINGTON sign seale & publish the above mentioned to be his last Will & Testament & that he was in parfect sence and memory at the Signing Sealing & publishing thereof to the best of your deponts. judgment

　　　　　　　　　　　　　　　　HENRY TANDY
Juratus est HENRICUS TANDY in Cur Com Rappa Sexto die Junii An 1677
p Sacram probatr et recordatr
　　　　　　　　　Test EDMD. CRASK Cl Cur

Memorandum
That what is contained in this Book from ye page 114 to this place is truely transcribed out of part of ye Book No. F and faithfully Examined by me this vith day of July MDCCXXXI

W. BEVERLEY Cl Cur

I, WILMER L. HALL, State Librarian of the Commonwealth of Virginia, do hereby certify that the foregoing pages contained in this bound volume are true and correct photostatic copies of the contents of the following Book, Rappahannock County WILLS, DEEDS, etc No. 1 1665-1677, and that all the pages contained in the Original of said Book have been photostated and copies thereof are included in this volume pursuant to the provisions of Chapter 230 of the Acts of the General Assembly of Virginia for the year 1928.

Given under my hand and the official Seal of the State Library Board at Richmond, Virginia, this 30th day of November 1934

WILMER L. HALL
State Librarian

ELIZA WILSONs Marke is a cropt in both ears and a slit in the left ear and two notches under the Right ear
Recorded 10th Aprill 1665   Test R. D. Cl Cur

Page 109 (Transcript)
State of Virginia
County of Essex to Wit:

I HARRISON SOUTHWORTH Clerk of the County Court for the County aforesaid in the State of Virginia do certify that I have verified the foregoing by a comparison of the same with the original record book in my office, and that it is a true copy thereof
Given under my hand this 10 day of October 1892
HARRISON SOUTHWORTH Clerk

COCK. Nicholas 1.
COCKER. Thomas 73.
COGHILL. Alice 20; James 19, 20.
COLLINS. Thomas 72.
CONNIERS. Dennis 63.
CONSTABLE. Nicholas 9.
COOMBE. Abram 18; Archdall 20.
COOPER. John (Grocer-1); Thomas (will of-63).
COPELAND. Nicho. 35.
CORBYN. Henry 61; Mr. 24.
CORNEWELL. Peter 20, 60.
COUNTIES: Accomack 28, 29; Glocester 67;
 Isle of White 32; Lancaster 12, 20, 22, 24,
 44; Lower Norfolk 25, 26; Westmoreland 10.
COX. Arabella (Strachey) 67; Henry (will of-
 66), 67, 68; John 1; William 67.
CRASK. Edmund (Clerk of Court-42), 52, 63,
 66, 67.
CREEKS: Cedar 19; Cross 12; Farnham 4;
 Gilsons 40; Golden Vale 5, 6, 7, 11;
 Hodgkins 39; Moons 40; Moraticon 43;
 Occupation 22; Occupacy 12; Parrys 75;
 Peumondson 53; Piscatacon 13, 37; Piscata-
 way 75; Popemans 8; Rappa. 17;
 Richards 30; Tigners 15, 21; Totoskey 12,
 16, 17; Williamsons 17; Youngs 19.
CREIGHTON. Francis 9, 10, 29, 30;
 Henry 1, 9, 10, 29, 30, 33, 70.
CUMBERLAND. Robert 16.

DALE. Edward 32.
DANDY. John 3.
DANIEL. Hugh 24; Thomas 2; William 3, 42.
DAVIS. Dr. 24; Evan 31, 37; George 2, 9;
 Mary 3?; Robert (Clerk-1), 2, 5, 10, 13, 20,
 23, 24, 32, 33, 35, 36, 39, 41; William 43, 47.
DAWSON. John 51.
DAYES. Thomas 75.
DEANE. John 12, 15.
DENNETT. Sam 30.
DEYOUNG. Ann 46; Elizabeth 46; Honour 46;
 John (will of-46), 47; John (Younger) 46.
DIOS (DYOS). Thomas 10.
DOBSON. Edmund 54.
DOUGHTY (DOWTY). Enoch 1, 19, 35; Francis
 (Minister-14), 26, 35, 39; John 52.
DRACAS. Edward 73.
DREWITT. John (will of- 57).
DUDLEY. Richard 62, 63.
DUNNIVAN. Peter 43, 53.
DURRANT. Henry 69.

DYER. William 55.

EAID. Robert 76.
EAVENS. John 60.
EFFORD. Zachery 47.
EGELSTON. Hugh 24.
ELDER. Peter (will of-57); Peter (Younger) 57.
ELLIOT. Henry 34.
ELLVERD. Betty 77; Thomas (will of-77).
ELSHER. Mary 9.
ELTHERSON. Elathy 23.
ENGLAND: Bound for 48; Bristoll 64;
 Canterbury 16; Lime 61; London 1, 3, 32, 50;
 Washington's Land 78.
EPER. Thomas 3.
ERWIN. Ann 70; Thomas 62, (will of-70, 71).
ESSEX. Bridget 55; John 55.
EVANS. John 61.

FANTLEROY. Mary 24; Colo. Moor 30.
FARREL. Thomas 20.
FENNELL. John 29.
FLEMING. Alexander 1, 5, 6, 7, 10, 11, 12, 14,
 19, 21, 26, 33, 36, 66; Capt. Alexander 8, 28,
 29, 38; Elizabeth 19; Capt. Lawrence 78;
 Ursula 28, 29.
FLOOD. Samuel 55.
FLOWER. Elias 40.
FOGGE. William 68.
FRANCE. John 18.
FREEMAN. Edward 76.
FRESHWATER. Thomas 1, 10, 13, 17, 18, 30, 39,
 40, 41, 46, 57, 64, 70.
FRISTO. David 45; Robert 4, 5.
FULLER. Alice 31.
FULLERTON. Elizabeth 8; James 1, 8, 9.

GAINES. Daniel 8, 49, 50, 51, 53, 54; John 29.
GARNER. John 74.
GARRETT. Anthony 17.
GATEWOOD. John 19.
GIBSON. John 53; William 1.
GILLET. John 6, 19.
GILSON. Andrew 40.
GLASCOCKE. Grigy 39; John 40; Thomas 39.
GLOVER. Richard 32, 38, 57.
GOODRICH. Charles 19; Thomas 14, 23, 26;
 Lt. Colo. Thomas 19, 39.
GOODRIG. John 22; Rebecca 22.
GOODYEAR. Robert 1, 22, 32.
GOOSE 24; Thomas 25.

GORDON. Jane 67; Thomas 67.
GOUDG. John 59.
GOULDMAN. Thomas 55.
GOVERNOR: Berkeley 8, 11, 12; Morrison 13.
GOWER. Richard 3.
GRANGER. W. 34.
GRAY. Abner 51, 52; John 51; Mary 52;
  Maudlin 52; Warwick 51; William (will
  of-51), 52; William (Younger) 51.
GRAYDON. Ralph 48.
GREEN. Roger 31.
GRIFFIN. Jesper 17; Leroy 4; Samuel 4, 12,
  17, (Merchant-25), 33; Thomas 25;
  Thomas (Elder) 25.
GRIGORY. John 14, 39; Capt. 74; John
  Junr. 73, 74; Richard 74.
GRIMSTED. Richard 61.
GRINSIN. Robt. 20.
GULLOCK. James 1; Jane 8.

HACKREY. Henry 56.
HALL. Mr. 44; William 26.
HARDESTY. John (will of-47), 48; Mary 48.
HARDING. William 65.
HARPER. Thomas 38, 63, 76.
HARRIS. John 32.
HARRISON. James 56.
HARROD. Martha 60; Mathew 60; Peter 60.
HART. Thomas 68.
HARWAR. Elizabeth 73; Thomas 27, 28, 72, 73.
HASELOCKE. George 11, 12.
HASLEWOOD. Henry 1; John 67.
HAWKINS. Capt. 24; Mary 54; Thomas 12, 14,
  20, 23, 25, 26, 31, 35, 38, 50, 54, 68, 78.
HERBERT. Andrew 25, 39; Clemt. 19.
HICKMAN. Fra. 15.
HILL. Robert 24, 25.
HINES. Richard 3; Thomas 60.
HINKSMAN. John 26.
HOBBS. John 40.
HODGES. Arthur 46; Mary 61; William 68.
HODGKINS. Phebe 48; William 9, 24, 27, 28,
  32, 33, (will of-48).
HODGSON. William 33.
HOGGE. Will. 29.
HOLT. Dorothy 7, 8; Elizabeth 46.
HOPGOOD. Peter 46, 73.
HORVESLEY. John 64.
HOWELL. George 4, 57.
HOWES. John 17.
HUDNALL. David 43.

HUDSON (HUTSON). Dorothy 46;
  Edward 22, (will of-45), 46.
HUGELL. Michael 23.
HULL. Elizabeth 71; John 11, 13, 22, 25;
  Capt. John 12, 47; Lt. Coll. John (will of-71),
  72; Roger 47, 71.

INDIANS: Nansatigmond Town 19;
  Nansemond Town 19; Path 29.
INGRAM. Thomas 52; Toby 52.
IXEM. Fredericke 32, 33.

JACKSON. George (will of-76).
JACOB. John 3, 4.
JAMES. Edward (will of-64), 65; John 35;
  Richard 2; Thomas 33.
JAMES CITY: 8, 11, 14, 15, 19, 27, 41, 55.
JEFFRIES. Mr. 50.
JENKINS. Francis 60; Thomas 2, (will of-76).
JENNIFER. Jacob 37.
JENNINGS. Francis 60.
JOHNSON. Martin 61; Peter 12, 13, 15;
  Samuel 43.
JOLLY. John 76.
JONES. Avis 63; Edward 70; Griffin 15;
  Jane 63; John 57, 63, 69, 74; John Junr. 74;
  Leonard 17; Richard 25, 26, 63;
  Richard (Younger) 63.

KAY. James 51.
KELLY. John 52; Mathew 52.
KENNY. Wm. 30.
KEYE. Frances 55.
KILMAN. George 13; John 1, 13; William 13.
KING. Richard 60.
KIRK (KERKE). Randal 13; Thomas 51.
KIRKMAN. Fr. (Cl. Cur) 18, 27.
KNIGHT. Richard 23.
KNOTT. George 46.

LAMPART. John 5, 6, 7, 10, 11, 15, 35.
LANDMAN. William 10
LANE. William 2, 21, 26, 34, (Merchant-35).
LANNE. Thomas 33.
LAWRENCE. Richard 23, 24, 25, 31, 36.
LAWSON. Joshua 55.
LEALUR. Bartholomew 69; Bartholomew
  (Younger) 69; John 69.
LEE. Collonel 44; John 33; Richard 33.
LENTON. Anthony 64; Henry 64;
  Sarah (Swellivant)_ 64.

POWELL. Richard 3, 4; Thomas 21, 22.

PRICE. Joseph 73; William 76.

PROSSER. John 2, 5, 6, 7, 10, 11,
  Martha 6, 7, 11.

RAW. Mary 74.

RAWSON (RASON). Thomas 15, 16.

RECORDS: Old Record Book 41.

REDERFORD. Robert 68.

RREVES. Henry 32.

REIMAS. Peter 33.

REYLEY (RYLY). Edward 44; Miles 11.

RICHARDS. William 2.

RICHARDSON. Nathaniel 58; Roger 5, 11, 38.

RIVERS: Elizabeth 25, 26; Rappa: 8, 11, 17,
  19, 31, 37, 40, 44, 55, 61.

ROBERTS. Thomas 75, 76.

ROBINSON. Thomas 14, 17, 39.

ROGERS. John 43.

ROOSON. Thomas 21.

ROUZEE (ROWZIE). Edward 16, 20, 48, 50.

RUNS: Occupacy 51.

RUSSELL. Dr. 42; Elisha/Alisha (Billington)
  58; John (will of-62).

RYMAN. John 25.

RYMER. John 2.

SAMFORD. James 14, 30, 39, 64.

SAUNDERS. Phillip 21.

SAVADGE. William 29.

SAXON. Elizabeth 57; John 57.

SCORY. Willm. (Clerke-33).

SERGANT. John 28; William 62, 70.

SETTLE. Francis 25.

SHARP. Anne 73; John 27, 29, 73;
  Judith 29, 30, 73.

SHATFORD. John 29, 30.

SHEARES. Henry 42.

SHEERMAN (SHEREMAN). Anne 62; Jane 62;
  Martin 62; Quintan 32, 38, 39;
  Quintillian 25, (will of-62). Quintillian
  (Younger) 62.

SHERLOCK. Andrew 69, 70; Hanna 69;
  John Elder 19, (will of-69), 70; John
  (Younger) 19, 69.

SHIPHY. Daniel 54.

SHIPP. Joseph 74.

SHIPS: Returne 26.

SIBLY. John 17.

SILLIVANT (SWELLIVANT). Dennis 30, 35;
  Johanna 30, 31.

SILVESTER. Richard 19.

SIMMS. Katherine 23; Richard 59, (will of-72);
  Walter 23.

SISSON. Amy 38, 39; Robert 10, 17, 18, 25,
  38, 39.

SLANY. Saml. 32, (Grocer-33).

SLAUGHTER. Francis 49, 51.

SMART. Mr. 28; William 29.

SMITH. Henry 48; Robert 10; Thomas 72;
  Tobias 27.

SNEDE. Thomas 29.

SOPER. John 63.

SOUTHWORTH. Harrison 79.

SOVEREIGN: Charles the 2nd: 8, 21, 27, 43.

SPEARMAN. John 6, 7, 10.

SPEED. John 20, 34, (will of-60).

SPICER. William (Carpenter-22), 23.

STEGGE. Thomas 14.

STANFORD. Richard 20; Vinct. 22.

STANNOP. Isack 44.

STERNE. Francis 32, 33.

STEVENS. Tobias 30.

STOAKES. Richard 14; William (will of-58).

STONE. Francis 47; John 26, 58, 69.

STONEHILL. John (Clerke-33).

STOTT. Brian 44.

STRACHEY. William 67.

STRINGER. John 58.

STUBLESON. Stuble 15, 16.

SUMMERLAND. Rebecca 23.

SUTTLE. Francis 11, 18, 69.

SWAMPS: Chestucksent 14; Dragon 31, 37;
  Gunn 15; Maddisons 3.

SWELLIVANT. Cornelius (will of-52); Daniel 64;
  Dennis (will of-64); Dennis (Younger) 64;
  Joane 64; Sarah 64.

TACKET. James 61.

TALBOTT. Thomas 73; William 17, 69, 73.

TALIAFER. Ro: 11.

TANDY. Henry Junr. 78.

TARPLEY. John 24.

TAVERNOUR. Jo: 13.

TAYLOR. Richard 23.

THACHER. Elizabeth 43; Mathew 43;
  Silvester 2, 26, 43.

THOMAS. Edward 61; Simon 17.

THORNTON. William 56.

THORP(E). Tho: 38; William 60.

TILLERY. Henry 62, 63.

TOMLIN(S). Robert 1, 32.

www.ingramcontent.com/pod-product-compliance
Lightning Source LLC
Chambersburg PA
CBHW080339270326
41927CB00014B/3284